Once Upon A Life

Extracting the Beauty from the Beast

Written By:
Guadalupe Gonzalez

Printed in the United States of America

Published By:

by: D'Anointed Heart Book Ministry

CEO: Yneka Hathorn

©February 2024

All rights reserved.

ISBN: 9798877682702

All rights reserved. No portion of this book may be reproduced in any form without permission in writing from the publisher, except as permitted by U.S. copyright law.

Unless otherwise indicated, all Scripture quotations are taken from the KJV Version of the Bible.

Spring, TX

Dedication

This book is dedicated to the original beauty in my life, Teresa deJesus Gonzalez, and to all of her children.

To my children, Arianna Mayte, Nikolas Salomon, and Deadato Santino. Thank you for loving this beauty back to light every time this world tried to knock the heart out of me.

To all the beauties in the world, known and unknown.

Forewords:

I remember as a young girl sitting on the edge of my seat with excitement listening to my first-grade teacher read us books. Then, there was the time I would go over to my grandmother's house to listen to my aunts who were teachers, principals, and superintendents tell amazing and funny stories about the education system. And just like it was yesterday, I remember when I first started to receive revelation from the Bible, and I was in awe of the words of Christ and inspired by the life of others. As I flipped from page to page through the books of Daniel and Ezekiel, the examples of these great stories inspired me. Amazing stories like these aren't necessarily heard on a daily basis. So, when I come across an inspiring story, I count it a blessing.

A short while ago, I experienced yet another blessing.
Thanks to G.G. I have known G.G. for over 16 years. She and I were a part of the same church community that brought about transformation to both of our lives. I was extremely excited when she decided to pen her story in a book. Her story is extraordinary and authentic, and it shows forth the beauty of the Lord's deliverance and Love. This book doesn't allow you to put it down. LOL. Spiritual warfare is one of the most prevalent topics today. Although some people desire to hear about it, there are not many who experience it AND understand it.

As an author, playwright and high school teacher, I have read many, many books. The way her story is

uniquely written sets this book in a category of its own. This book not only teaches you about spiritual warfare, but it walks you through it using the lives of G.G. and three of her friends within an amazing concept. Although the concept may be fictional, the stories are not. NO DRAMA. NO LIES. NO FABRICATION. Just truth. There is not one person who would not be able to relate to at least one of the characters in this book.

If you are looking to read real life stories that depict the spiritual realm and want to find out how to overcome the different traumatic experiences that you have encountered, this is the book for you. As you read, you just may think that you are watching a movie. The imagery places you in the story, and you'll feel like you're taking the journey with them. After you have read the book, you will be excited about spiritual warfare and gain an understanding that it is nothing to fear. This book may be the answer to some of your prayers and long-standing questions. I only pray that you receive the excitement and understanding that I did when I read it. ENJOY!!!

Darriel Tanner

When a friend told me she was going to write a book about her life. I didn't expect her to have experienced such a tumultuous past. As the Gigi I have come to know reflects strength and is always looking out for those around her. In this story of her life's journey, she gives insight on how she became the woman she is today. As she mixes entertaining fiction with real life flashbacks, this book will help guide those who are also dealing with challenges in their life.

Heather Lopez

Once Upon A Life
Extracting the Beauty from the Beast

Table Of Contents

Introduction		pg. 8
Chapter 1	What's the Point?	pg. 12
Chapter 2	The Lay of The Land	pg. 24
Chapter 3	The Journey	pg. 36
Chapter 4	The Cycle	pg. 56
Chapter 5	Intersections & Detours	pg. 84
Chapter 6	The Climb	pg. 101
Chapter 7	Small Beginnings	pg. 126
Chapter 8	Closing In	pg. 139
Chapter 9	Deception	pg. 156
Chapter 10	Golden City	pg. 163
Chapter 11	Reversing The Curse	pg. 172
Chapter 12	Homecoming	pg. 199
About The Author		pg. 212

Introduction

At the mention of the words, fairy *tales*, images of good guys, bad guys, and princesses probably come to mind. As a kid, I absolutely loved fairy tales. Perhaps I loved them because of their beauty. Perhaps it was the aspect of good overcoming evil; more than anything it was witnessing someone's misfortune be overcome and the ending be full of happiness and beauty. Stories of overcoming often ffilled me up with hope. In fact, one of my all-time favorites was *Beauty and the Beast*. Perhaps I enjoyed the story so much because I could relate to how the beast felt. Not just in a physical sense, but environmentally as well. Although he did not have the best of circumstances, he ended up with his happy ending.

Unfortunately, the reality is that life doesn't always have a fairy tale ending. When one grows up in conditions that lack love, beauty and/or safety, one can easily become hardened and mean. This almost occurred within me, yet by The Grace of God, it did not. Growing up in an environment ffilled with violence and lack while still clinging to hope, quickly did two things within me:

1. *It conditioned me to remain in a constant mode of survival* and

2. *It made me incredibly grateful for any opportunity or kindness I encountered on my journey.*

It also caused me to pay attention to the people around me and how their choices impacted their lives and at times my own. I was not sure how, but I wanted and hoped for better. Better was good enough for me. Safer was good enough for me. Becoming better was my objective. Anytime I saw a way to do or become better, I learned how it was achieved and would soon be in the gainful pursuit of that goal. Along the way, I learned the art of perseverance, and how to safeguard my softness. However, my truth was that I wasn't just soft, I was also weak. I was ffilled with

fear, doubt, insecurity but simultaneously inspired by hope. Yet even despite the hope I clung to, at times when things got so tough,
I would often question, *Why fight? What am I fighting for? What is the point?*

It seemed that every metaphorical step forward I took, it would appear I would take ten hits back. What is a hit? A hit is something that takes away or hurts you financially, emotionally, mentally, or spiritually. It was a beastly cycle—that is, until I gained a true revelation of Jesus Christ. It was then that I started to understand *Spiritual Warfare* and began to gain ground permanently.

People must understand that the challenges we encounter in life are always rooted in a spiritual battle. Jesus is not make-believe or a pretend story that Christians have made up to entertain ourselves.

There are spiritual entities that are strategizing and battling day and night for you're the components of our soul and those of our bloodlines. Spiritual warfare is real.

What is your soul? I heard a wise man, Dr. James Pierce, state, "A soul is a compilation of your mind, will, emotions, intellect, and imagination."

There is a battle between heaven and hell for your mind, will, emotions, intellect, and imagination. Let me paraphrase that again: There is a sustained, outright violent fight to obtain or invade the components of your soul—between two large, organized armed forces belonging to Heaven and Hell. Angels and demons are fighting relentlessly, fiercely, and violently for your soul.

Before we were even conceived, God had a plan for us.

<u>Jeremiah 29:11 says, 'For I know the plans I have for you,' declares the Lord, 'plans to prosper you and not to harm you, plans to give you hope and a future.'</u>

However, during our life's journey the enemy comes to steal, kill, and destroy that plan by enslaving our minds, poisoning our imaginations, weakening our wills, destroying our emotions, and keeping us ignorant.

Often the battle for our soul begins when we are children and completely ignorant of spiritual laws. Our childhood is supposed to be a time of innocence, wonder and development; yet often this is the time when the enemy or the demons of hell push the hardest to take the greatest advantage over us. Many times, due to our parents' ignorance, we may find ourselves vulnerable, and exposed. This is when seeds of hurt from physical, sexual, and verbal abuse are planted deep within our hearts, and wrong mindsets are ingrained.

For many of us, the beauty in life that was predestined for us is lost or hindered because we are already inheriting bloodlines that have been depleted of Gods blessings due to losses of those who came before us and also because we are steadily losing spiritual battles, we have no idea we are even engaged in. This vicious cycle will continue to the lives of our children and our children, until someone says "This curse ends on the cross through MY faith. I AM that

one!" *<u>Hosea 4:6 states that we are destroyed for a lack of knowledge</u>*. What we don't know could hurt us.

My purpose in writing this book is to assist those in understanding spiritual warfare, to offer hope to those who find themselves hopeless, to extract the beauty that God intended for our lives amidst beastly situations, and to show you, through my journey, how I began to take back territory the Beast had stolen from my bloodline and myself. My desire is to help others establish and obtain generational blessings, break generational curses, and strengthen lineages in Christ while gaining more souls for His Kingdom.

In 1920, L. Frank Baum authored a story with a great concept about a young girl and her dog taking a journey to receive directions to get back home, after they had been caught in a tornado and thrown into an unknown land. On this journey, the girl met three other people who needed help also, so they decided to take the journey together. They experienced much opposition; however, they also received assistance and ultimately found what they were in search of. If you haven't already recognized the book I am referring to, it is titled, *The Wonderful Wizard of Oz*

Just like the young girl, Dorothy and her three friends, we are all on journeys. We want to live out our dreams and fulfill our potential. Others of us are heaven bent on breaking generational curses and attaining the blessings for our families. In this life, we will experience trials, tribulations, and oppositions that are set to deter us from our God ordained destinations. However, there is also help—I like to call it divine assistance and connections—in the form of a loving Savior, great mentors, family, and friends who come to our rescue.

My journey has not been easy, but I can say that this is my story, and every experience has helped me to be the woman I am today. Join me as I share moments and special people who God utilized as He extracted this beauty from the beast, once upon a life.

Chapter 1

What's the Point?

As soon as I walked onto the unit, Heather walked over to me and said, "Hey, Ms. Hawkins is here, and she's looking for you."

"What? Ugh. For me? Now what?" I asked.

I purposely had been trying to avoid Ms. Hawkins, the manager, due to past run ins.

"Girl, I think we're short today," Heather said, with wide eyes as she walked away.

I took a deep breath and quickly adjusted my stethoscope as I continued to organize myself for the shift.

"Thank you, God," I whispered again as I made a conscious decision to stay grateful no matter what.

As I stepped into the first patient's room with Heather to give a report, I looked over to my right and saw a thin African American female wearing a bright pink handkerchief on her head.

Heather began, "Ms. Fanci was admitted two days ago for a left-sided breast mass."

Then Heather lowered her voice and began to whisper, "We just found out the mass is malignant. The doctors will be here in the morning to inform her and to discuss treatment options." Then, increasing her volume again, she said,
"Our main goal today is to manage her pain."

I nodded my head as I heard a knock at the door.

"Hi, Ms. Hawkins," I said as I noticed the supervisor standing in the doorway. I had only been out of precepting for about a month, and from the beginning she made it clear she had been against my placement on this unit.

"G.G., after you get done with this report, I need to see you at the nurses' station," Ms. Hawkins stated prior to walking away.

"Yes ma'am. No problem," I replied.

I took a deep breath and shrugged my shoulders. I could feel the tension rising in my body, and my heart began to race throughout the remainder of Heather's report. I headed over to the nurses' station.

"We are pulling you down to the third floor, G.G.," Ms. Hawkins informed me.

"That can't be right. I was just pulled last week." I said.

I reached over the counter and grabbed the schedule.

The third floor was where they stuck the hospital's overflow. It was commonly understaffed, and the lowest man on the totem pole was often placed there. I knew it was somebody else's turn.

"It's not my turn. It's Phoebe's turn," I said as I looked over at Phoebe, who rolled her eyes.

Then Phoebe responded, "I'm not going downstairs. You're the newbie." She flipped her hair as she headed into another patient's room.

"G.G., it's not open for discussion. Please gather your things and go downstairs," Ms. Hawkins said.

My breathing began to speed up, and I could feel my adrenaline begin to kick in. I stood there leaning on the counter of the nurses' station and closed my eyes.

"G.G., please gather your things and head downstairs because we are short," said Ms. Hawkins.

As the anger grew within me, I slowly walked over to gather my materials. She trailed behind me.

Underneath my breath, I whispered, "Holy Spirit, please help me stay in control."

"GG, are you saying something? If you have something to say, speak up," Ms. Hawkins said as she smacked her teeth.

She continued to speak to me a little more harshly as we walked away from the nurses' station.

"Let's put things into perspective, you do have the option of going home and choosing to take a write-up for insubordination," said Ms. Hawkins.

As she was speaking, I began to have a flashback of a time in my life that I had long since forgotten …

The Fight

"G.G., go to the store and get me a pack of cigarettes," my mom said as she handed me some money.

"OK Mami," I responded. I was 8 years old, and it was summer break. I put the change she had given me carefully into my pocket, and I ran out the front door. Mentally, I began to prepare for this journey. Within seconds, the pavement was burning the soles of my feet as I ran to the store. Quickly, I developed a pattern that would make the path more tolerable. I ran from tree shade to shade, allowing my feet to cool down before I tackled another stretch of the hot pavement. On the way, I saw the neighbor girls playing at the park. Though these girls could be mean. Occasionally, they could be nice. I decided to take a chance.

"Hey guys, what are y'all doing?" I asked.

"We're playing," they said.

"Can I play too?" I asked.

"No," they said.

"Why?" I asked.

Then one of the girls whispered into the ear of the other, and they erupted in laughter.

"What's funny?" I asked as I started swinging next to them anyway.

"We don't want to play with you because your mom's a b****," said Onya.

My facial expression changed.

"No, she's not!" I yelled as I jumped off the swing.

"Uh-huh, my dad says so," she yelled.

"You better quit calling my mom that," I said as I started to get angry and began to walk up on her.

She responded, "I can say whatever I want. Your mom is a b****."

"I told you not to say that again!" I yelled.

Then I punched her in the face as hard as I could. Blood squirted out of her nose, and she started crying. Her cousin quickly grabbed her and led her away, saying, "We're telling."

Vindicated, I quickly finished my journey to the store and returned home. When I returned, I handed my mom her cigarettes. She was lying on the bed, reading her tarot cards. "Go light it up on the stove for me, mija," she said. I grabbed the cigarette and began telling her what happened at the park as I bent over the stove and puffed on the cigarette to light it up.

"People are always going to talk. Let them. They don't pay my bills," she said.

Just then, there was a knock at the door. It was Onya, holding a tissue over her nose, still crying with her father at her side.

"Let me talk to your mom," he demanded. Intimidated, I walked over to my mom's room and told her. My mom quickly changed out of her nightgown and threw some clothes on. When she arrived, the man began to complain, "Your daughter punched my daughter in the nose, and she shouldn't have done that." Everyone looked down at me for a response. I stared at Onya and her father, and I confessed.

"Yes, I did hit her, but it's because she was calling my mom names, and I warned her," I started to get angry, and my eyes began to tear up.

He replied, "You had no right to hit my daughter. Lady, you need to watch your daughter."

I responded, "No, your daughter needs to stop talking about my mom."

Then the man began to raise his voice even louder. "Your daughter owes my daughter an apology!" he yelled.

"No," I responded, "I am not apologizing. For what?" Onya's father began to grow angry, and he continued yelling. At this point my mom intervened. She looked down at me and said, "G.G., apologize." It felt as if someone had just smacked me full force in the face.

I looked at her and said, "Mom, that's not right. I warned her. No, mom."

"G.G., apologize now," she repeated. My eyes filled up with tears, but I refused to cry in front of these people. This man and his daughter had insulted my mom, and I reacted. Yet I had to apologize. I was filled with anger at the injustice. Reluctantly, I obeyed my mother.

"I'm sorry, Onya," I said.

I began to envision myself lunging at Ms. Hawkins when I was quickly brought back to the sound of a familiar voice.

"Hey GG, you forgot this." My coworker, Mary, walked toward us, holding my clipboard, she placed her arm over my shoulders and encouraged me toward the elevators a few feet ahead.

I could feel Ms. Hawkins gaze upon us as we stepped into the elevators and watched the doors close. I looked down and my eyes watered.

"Hey, it's OK," Mary said and rubbed my shoulder. "Get through this shift, and we can take it up with admin in the morning, shake it off," she said.

I nodded my head, took a deep breath, and wiped my face. "You're right," I said as I hugged her.

Just then the elevator bell dinged, and the doors opened. Waiting right outside the doors was Joe, the tech in Army green scrubs mouthing, "She's yours." He looked down and began pushing a wheelchair holding a woman who appeared to have been physically assaulted. Her eyes were blackened, and her lip was still bleeding. Her hair was disheveled. As I walked out, they made their way into the elevator. I turned to look at the patient one more time, and her hazel eyes locked mine, and I gave her a warm smile.

After a few seconds, I turned around and headed toward the unit I had been assigned. Surely it was going to be a long night.

Much to my surprise, though it was busy it surprisingly went by quickly. Towards the end of my shift, I headed to the break room for a cup of coffee. I thought about my patients and everything they had going on and suddenly I was filled with gratitude for my life.

As I sipped on my coffee, I also thought about my problems with Ms. Hawkins, and I was even more grateful that I hadn't snapped. I decided I would head straight home after my report and see how this thing with Ms. Hawkins played itself out.

Later, as I sat in my car waiting for it to heat up. As I began reflecting on my journey, flashbacks of the smoldering pavement that day at the park came back to me. I took a deep breath and whispered, "Thank you God." Every time I reflect on the challenging moments of my life and the lessons that were acquired; I am filled with gratitude.

Shady Business

Shortly after Onya and her father left, I sat in the living room quiet and overwhelmed with emotions I did not understand. A brief time later, my mother asked me to brush my hair and put on my shoes because we were going to the store. I was surprised, as my mom would often opt to leave us kids at home while she ran errands. However, on this day, for the first time ever, my mom and I were going to the store, just the two of us.

I remember sitting in the front seat with her. I was so happy just to be with her. When we got down to the local market, she turned to me and said, "G.G., get one thing."

I looked over at her. I was shocked. "What?" I asked.

She repeated, "Get one thing."

My mouth dropped as this type of thing had never happened before. I quickly ran around the store looking for my one thing. As soon as I selected my prize I headed over to the checkout lanes to find her. I smiled as I looked into her eyes and handed her my gift. Her eyes quickly revealed a new emotion, and though I could not understand it completely then, I quickly understood that my gift was a reward. That day I promised myself that I would always fight for my mom, and furthermore, I would fight for anyone who was too weak, too afraid, or too far gone to fight for themselves.

In my car that morning after my shift, I let out a big sigh and laid back my head on the headrest. My journey had been long. Suddenly, a memory came rushing in. I was in the 6th grade and trying hard to find a shirt to wear for picture day. That year there had been no new clothes for school, but picture days were a big deal. I remember anxiously walking over to my friend's house hoping she'd let me borrow a shirt. I had recently found out the age requirement to get a job, and that day I promised myself that as soon as I turned 16, I would get a job and work so much that I would always be able to afford my own clothes. My life would be better.

I turned on the heater and leaned over to hit the defrost button. Though I definitely had accomplished better since my childhood, I was still having to work 80+ hours a week at times, as a single parent, for that *better*, and Ms. Hawkins was stressing me out on top of it. I was being challenged to step up towards an even-better future, but I was simultaneously trying to heal from my past.

"Dear Jesus, help me."

I took another deep breath of the ice cold air and blew my warm breath onto my hands, impatiently waiting for my car to heat up. I noticed my hot pink tote peeking up at me from the passenger seat. I reached over into the bag and pulled out the mask I had worn at a recent masquerade ball. I ran my fingers over the top of it. I smiled as I remembered how excited I was for this event. It was an opportunity for me to doll up from head to toe, as opposed to my daily scrub wear. During this reception, I was honored with an award, and during the speech I delivered, I made sure I did my best to set the bar high as my children were watching. I hoped they would remember this day as a point to level up in their own lives. I loved this mask not just for its beauty but for the memories it stirred up within me. It was a reminder to me that anything is possible. I stared at the mask for a little longer, and then I gently put it back.

I reached around and felt other items in my bag: my Success Journal, my favorite pink pen, and a book. I placed the bag on the seat next to me, and I shifted the gear. I had been trying for the past few years to become who I was predestined to be. "Whatever that is," I said to myself. I still didn't know who that was entirely yet. I had been working so hard to improve in every area of my life, and it was not easy. This just wasn't fair. I had grown up with all the odds stacked up against me. "Lord," I asked, "when is enough, enough? What else can you possibly want from me?"

The thoughts continued to run through my mind. Memories of my interactions with Ms. Hawkins the previous night began to resurface. I also thought of all the different obstacles I had to overcome just to get to this place and instantly, I felt like that little girl from the projects all over again. Anger began to rise as my eyes watered. "Why does this always happen to me? What's the point?" I thought.

I pulled out of the parking lot and turned up the music to drown out my thoughts. The anger I had been suppressing was beginning to surface and then I released it.

"What's the point, God? TELL ME!" I yelled out. I had worked hard my whole life ... suddenly I heard cars honking as I hit a large piece of black ice, and my car started to spin in circles, out of control. I screamed at the top of my lungs "Jesus!" Then, as if going in slow motion, the car came to a slow stop.

Chapter 2

The Lay of the Land

After a few minutes, I had managed to calm myself down and though nothing appeared to have changed, I sensed that something was different.

I wiped the fog from the driver's side window with the sleeve of my shirt and looked outside. Was I hallucinating? Did I die? Did I have a concussion?

Lo and behold, it looked like paradise. There wasn't any sign of snow anywhere. There were bright green fields resting on each side of the road covered with blankets of colorful flowers. The buildings were brightly colored, and there was so much beauty all around me. The roads were made of rose gold colored cobble stone and the entire scene encouraged a sense of peace. At first, I was apprehensive to get out of the car but eventually, the smell of wild jasmine and cotton candy lured me out. I slowly stepped out of the car and checked my surroundings. I was unsure if I should proceed further. Then, I closed my eyes and took a deep breath, and the scent of jasmine flooded my senses. I was stirred to a feeling of safety and decided to take a few more steps.

As I looked around I noticed seating arrangements spread out in various places. There were colorful benches and swings that seemed to hang from the sky. Each added its own unique accent that flowed with the beautiful scenery. There were big screens everywhere with some kind of reality show on display and there were 2 huge waterfalls that flow powerfully and freely. Their synchronized sounds enhanced the esthetics of the land.. I continued to follow the rose gold path a little further when suddenly I saw a figure fast approaching from one of the brick roads.

As the figure neared, I realized it was a woman clothed in a beautiful floral dress. She had a few blonde streaks flowing throughout her light brown hair, which was long and thick. Her makeup was intact, and she held the poise of a queen. "Hello, beautiful girl. It's alright. We've been waiting on you for quite some time. My name is Stacia," she said.

"Wait, did you say 'we'? What do you mean by 'we'?" I asked.

I began to look around, when out of nowhere different circles of crystal lights began to appear. As they drew closer, they began to form into human-like figures. Some of them had what appeared to be wings attached to their backs. Some of them were so small they could fit in the palm of my hand while others were as tall as the buildings located throughout this land I found myself in. I stared in awe. I had heard about angels and had a few dreams, but I wasn't quite sure what I was looking at.

I looked around, and I could feel my legs shaking. Then, a familiar cool presence came upon me, but this time it grew more intense. I could barely stand. The next thing I knew I was laid out on the floor.

As the feeling diminished, I began to sit up and said, "God bless America.." This expression had become a staple in my vocabulary and served as a substitute for words that weren't quite blessings,
"Excuse me; I'm not sure what came over me."

Stacia then gave me a warm smile, held out her hand and said, "I do."

"That was the Holy Spirit. Normally He is quite the gentleman, but He does have that effect at times," she said as she let out a chuckle.

As I was carefully assisted back to my feet I asked, "What are they?"

Then, I quickly closed my mouth as it had dropped open with a mixture of astonishment and some disbelief.

Stacia laughed and said, "They are angels. To be more precise, they are your angels, and they are here to help you because you are a born-again believer. They are specifically assigned to help you throughout your lifetime. In fact, all around here you will find different kinds of angels; now, these aren't all yours, of course. She let out a chuckle. However, you do have a band of angels assigned specifically to you, of course.

Unfortunately, quite a few of these guys end up hanging out here looking for work often, because so many believers aren't even aware they exist, much less of how to access their power."

Just then I looked over, and I recognized an elderly man with a cane who looked remarkably familiar. He stepped out and winked at me. Then a memory came rushing back.

Ministering Spirits

I didn't grow up like a typical kid. Despite being around so many people, I grew up very alone. On one particular day when I was 3 years old, and found myself alone and unattended in the back of a pickup truck. Initially, I had barely taken notice and had been distracted playing, but after some time, I began to get scared and began to cry out for my mother. Suddenly, out of nowhere, a little old man with a cane appeared. He walked over and tipped his hat at me, revealing a head of white hair, and though he smiled, his face was filled with concern. "Don't cry little one, you're going to be OK," he said. He reassured me momentarily, then headed back into the store. When he returned, he came out with a big brown paper bag filled with candy.

He handed it to me and winked and said, "It's all for you. Try one."

I opened one and soon became so busy opening the next wrapper that I had forgotten I was upset.

As I popped the second piece of candy into my mouth and looked up, he was gone. I looked everywhere, but he seemed to have magically disappeared.

Quickly, I snapped out of it, and the elderly figure with the can smiled at me.

"Do you remember him?" Stacia asked and then stated, "That's Ethan. He doesn't really need a cane. That is his earth suit. He brought it out today when he heard you were coming. He felt it would help you remember, and he thinks it makes him more approachable." Then Stacia winked her eye at Ethan

I looked around in amazement as more angels began to appear. I hadn't realized there were so many of them. Some were sitting , some were flying in and out of the waterfalls and others were looking at the large screens as if they were watching a movie.

As I looked closer at one of the screens, one of the characters caught my attention. She was being bullied by another girl, and she wasn't doing anything to defend herself. Perhaps it was the almond-shaped eyes, but suddenly it hit me—it was my daughter.

"Hey, what is this?" I exclaimed.

Stacia looked over to the screen and then over to a blond-haired angel. "Eric, go," said Stacia as she pointed over at the screen.

Ethan quickly picked up his cane and moved towards an opening in the center of it all. "I'll go with him," Ethan said. It seemed angels were descending and ascending on a staircase. As they grew closer to the top, Eric and Ethan began to disappear.

"That's our version of reality TV: real people and real time. She'll be fine. Don't worry. They will not fail," said Stacia.

Then suddenly it grew a little dark, and I began to smell a stench. "What is that smell?" I asked as I plugged up my nose.

"That, er, smells like Jez," said Stacia as she pinched her nose as well.

A woman appeared, dressed in all black. She resembled Ms. Hawkins. But this figure's eyes and countenance were extremely dark.

"Jez, how many times have I expressed the importance of bathing daily—multiple times if you can—and don't be scared of ample deodorant either," said Stacia as she continued to hold her nose and frown at the woman.

Jez walked slowly past Stacia toward me, as she stared at Stacia suspiciously.

"Well, you finally made it, G.G. It took you long enough. We too have been waiting for you." she said in an eerie voice.

"What are you doing over here with these folks? We have a spot reserved for you. You belong with us. I heard Stacia call you beautiful," she started to laugh, "but you and I both know who you really are and the things you've done," she said, laughing out loud. "You can't fool me," she said. She eyes me from head to toe.

Then she looked over at Stacia. "You have the wrong girl," Jez snarled, and then she swiftly closed in on me, sneering and sniffing around my face like a vicious dog.

"You want to know who you are, do you? That's easy," she said as she quickly moved from side to side, abnormally close, closely inspecting every curve of my face.

"Where do you come from? THINK about it! The apple NEVER falls far from the tree, and we ALL know what and who you come from. G.G., there is nothing worthy or honorable running through your DNA. Generation after generation of your bloodline has run with my pack for years," said Jez as she took a step away from me.

"Do you really think you can break the bond of your bloodline with mine?" she laughed out loud.

"Your identity ... hmmm. Think about it, yes. Let's just THINK! There is no beauty in any of it.
Should we get going now or shall I start to inform Stacia about how you can't be trusted? How old were you when you stole the first time?" She demanded.

I knew exactly what Jez was talking about. It was true. I would never have used the word beautiful to describe anything about me or where
I came from. I came from darkness—ranging from infidelities, promiscuity, drugs, alcohol to tarot cards, tales of black magic, and witchcraft. Black magic deals with evil supernatural powers and spells performed to inflict harm or to control someone's will. Though we spoke of God, we were a people who ignorantly worshiped various, albeit modern, idols. We were plagued with poverty, anxiety, and fear. Aside from my mother who would take us to church on occasion, I had just begun my own journey with God recently. 'She was right' I thought. My eyes began to water as I thought, *Who the heck am I?*

Overwhelmed with guilt, I began to walk toward Jez when suddenly I heard these words:

"In Jesus' name, you have no power here! Get out of here, Jez. I rebuke you. In Jesus Name. She belongs here now, and she will get everything she needs right on time. It is ALL working for her good according to Romans 8v28," encouraged Stacia, motioning me over with her hands.

At the sound of her words, Jez flew backward as if she had been socked in her belly, and she fell to the ground with an audible thud.

Jez struggled to stand on her feet but quickly began to move towards me again. Stacia moved over next to me and placed her hand on my shoulder.

"You won't always be there to protect her, Stacia, and when you aren't around, I swear that I will be," said Jez, looking straight into my eyes. "I'll see you around."

Suddenly she vanished into thin air.

Stacia turned and looked at me. She knew that I was concerned but I was also curious. "What made her fly back like that?"

"Oh, That. Girl, that was what we call a Holy Blow. The Word of God will always deliver injury to the enemy when used faithfully. These hits will render your enemy powerless for a time and at times even permanently. I know that this is all new to you, in this land that is how you deal with your enemies. G.G., you have been questioning your identity for quite some time. You've had a rough life, and you have responded to some of those things based on who you thought you were, but it's time for you to walk in the fullness of who God created you to be. When you accepted and acknowledged Jesus Christ as your personal Savior, you inherited a new bloodline. A bloodline overflowing with protection, blessings and nobody can ever take this away from you. It was paid for by the blood that Jesus shed on Calvary." said Stacia.

Still in shock and uncertain of what she was saying, I asked, "What is this place called?"

"This place is called the Land of Purpose. People come here at different points of their life. Some people are like you and want to know who they really are, others need help, or love and others run into this place accidentally." She smiled, "well at least for them it seemed accidental, but everything was predestined. Nothing is ever really a coincidence in life

"Well, how do I find out *my* identity and *my* purpose?" I asked.

"You have to go see Yo Soy El Que Soy," she said.

After she mentioned His name, the angels bowed and began to call out to each other saying "Holy, Holy, Holy."

"Who?" I whispered.

She repeated "Yo Soy El Que Soy."

The angels repeated again, "Holy, Holy, Holy."

"Yes, that's His Name. He has many names but around here we call him, Mr. El. and he has all your answers," said Stacia.

"How do I find Him?" I asked.

"He's in the Golden City ... it's a secret place," said Stacia.

"How do I get there?" I asked.

"Well," she looked over at my car, which appeared to be in its own distress, albeit mechanically. It looks like you will have to walk. All you in the forefront of your mind, and remember, it's all working out for your good." said Stacia.

Then I started to look around.

She continued, "Jez and the others will come for you. They will do everything to try to get you off track. On your way, you will see, hear, and experience many unusual things, emotions and thoughts. You must keep moving. Don't get distracted. Do not get detoured. This journey draws out the good and the not so good inside your heart. Keep your destination in the forefront of your mind. You must keep moving forward. Stay on the narrow,
white road, and remember you are not alone, beautiful girl."

As Stacia departed, some of the angels went with her, and others lingered.

"But Stacia, what about my daughter?" I asked. It was too late. Stacia had already disappeared.

I began to worry about my daughter when Ethan began to descend from above, and he smiled warmly at me.

"She's safe at home now, but you have quite the journey ahead of you," said Ethan.

He pointed to the narrow white road with his cane, and I knew exactly what he meant. It was time to take a journey.

Chapter 3

The Journey

There was something different about this road. Even the white, well it was a different type of white. I never knew white could be so, well, white.

As I began to walk, I began to reflect on the events that had transpired so far. Everything just seemed so surreal. Yet, there was something about Stacia that I trusted. Her words brought me hope, and although I didn't fully understand, I knew that when I reached the end of the narrow white road, I would meet Mr. El. Then I would find my true identity and quickly return home to my family.

I started walking as I replayed Stacia's instructions in my mind.

Suddenly, I saw my shiny hot pink tote lying on the ground beside the car. It was just a few feet in front of me.

It must've fallen out at some point, I thought. I ran over and picked it up. I quickly reached inside of it, and I could feel my mask. I carefully pulled it out to assess any damage. There was a hairline crack running down one side.

Great, I thought as I stared at it.

This mask was symbolic to me of what I could become, and now it was destroyed. Frustrated, I threw it to the side of the road.

Then I heard someone say, "Hey, don't do that."

I looked around, but I didn't see anybody. "Great," I said, "now I'm hearing things."

I threw up my hands in the air, and as they flopped back down to my sides, I heard, "Excuse me, but do pick me up, and try to be a little more careful. I may prove to be useful to you on this journey—after all, I do know a few things about this place."

I traced the voice back to the place where I had thrown the mask and slowly walked over. I wasn't sure about what to expect, as I had already seen so many incredible things. As I looked down I saw my mask on the floor, but it, too, was different. The original designs on it had changed to a mixture of white and gold. It said, "Yes, young lady. I believe I may be of assistance to you yet."

The mask was talking to me. I face-palmed myself and said, "Is this really happening?
God bless America."

"Oh, He will," the mask said, "because you said it, and in your tongue lies the power of life and death. But for now, I'm going to need you to pull yourself together and pick me up, please. We are wasting time, and we really do have places to go."

I slowly bent down to pick up the mask, and it began speaking. "OK, so let me explain to you how this is going to work. My name is Doc, and I know this place like the back of my hand. Well—if I had hands, of course," Doc chuckled to himself.

"But if you listen to me, I will show you the way to go. There are things in this land that you can't see because your eyes aren't trained to see them, yet. But I can see because I'm a veteran to this land. Some of the things going on here can be pretty scary, and not everyone can deal with them, so you may not want to see. But if at any point you think you are ready, then just pull me over your face. I will show you the spiritual reality of this land, even as we stand here."

"You just have to promise you are going to be more careful, young lady as I have already taken a hit during your little re-enactment of *The Fast and the Furious* in your car earlier," he said as he looked up to the right side of the mask.

I carefully placed the mask over my face.

Instantly, the beautiful scenery I had been seeing was converted into a battlefield. The entire place was covered in dark gray and black areas throughout. The flowers were gone, and different pits of fire and flames were dispersed throughout the land. The angels I had seen earlier were battling with what appeared to be shadows and skeleton figures. Encircling me were foggy areas, and some of the fog appeared to form various shapes of darkened figures. My angels were fighting fiercely. Some were hand to hand fighting, and others waged their war with swords. Yet amidst all this darkness, the road I stood on continued to shine brightly with an awesome glow.

Just then, I noticed one of the larger dark figures turning toward me and approaching at an abnormally rapid pace. As it reached out to grab me, a huge metal sword came from behind me and struck it down. Astonished, I stepped forward quickly and spun around so that I could see the bearer of the sword.

My jaw dropped as I saw, not one, but hundreds of angels flying behind me, and quickly surrounding me in a huddle like formation. From a distance, the place I was at in the narrow white path surrounded by all the darkness was comparable to a light bulb burning in the dark night. But in place of insects eagerly seeking the light, there were dark demons trying to put mine out. Quickly, I yanked off the mask and just as I was about to throw it down, I heard Doc say, "Hey there; hey you, young lady. Don't do that," smacking his lips.

Just in time, I secured the mask and quickly looked around. The butterflies and rainbows had returned. In the distance, I could hear the crash of the waterfalls, and the beauty of the place soon began to soothe my anxiety

"What was that!?!" I yelled, as I jumped up

Doc began to speak, "I told you not everyone can handle the Truth, but it is essential for you to know what you are up against if you are to truly learn of your identity. I know it's a lot to take in, but we really do have to get going. You can choose to "see," and I can help you walk in The Truth, or you can carefully situate me back until my guidance is needed, to prevent further incidents with the integrity of my composition. Bag and pull me out as you need me. Regardless of what you choose, we have to get going."

I placed the mask back over my eyes just in time to catch another glimpse of a demon coming at me. Quickly, I pulled it away from my face and back in the bag it went.

"Thanks Doc, but this is all a bit much for me right now," I said.

"Well, OK, but I am here. Please remember to be cautious of how you are handling your tote," he said.

I then continued on my journey, more aware.

On the path **of** The Narrow White Road were many street signs. I noticed the names of the cities and familiar streets. The names were both descriptive and unique.

On the way, a huge black sign with creepy red writing caught my eye. It read, "Welcome Home of All Generational Curses."

I immediately stopped and considered my options. I looked back. I really wasn't sure if I should proceed, but I didn't really have another choice. This was the only way forward. I had to find out who I was, and I had to get back home.

As I continued to walk, I came across a street. I looked up and it read the street sign out loud, "Teresa's Trauma." I turned so that I could see what was going on down that street and right before I crossed it, a vivid scene play out before me. Teresa was my mother.

Teresa's Trauma

Angry, the flames spread out, growing in ferocity as the fire engulfed the material possessions from a past life. She began counting her children again: "One, two, three, four, five, six, seven … one, two, three, four, five, six, seven …" She frantically began calling out her children's names. Someone was missing. Instantly she knew who it was. "G.G. … en donde está G.G.?" Realizing her 3-year-old was missing, Teresa began to turn back despite the heat from the intimidating flames. Then suddenly she heard, "Aqui estoy!"

The little girl shouted as she came running out of the front door wearing nothing more than her favorite red ruffled underwear. Teresa had just bathed her that night and carefully brushed out her long hair. They were all in their pajamas and had been in bed prior to this moment. Teresa stood there as her children gathered around her, huddling like a strategizing football team, but this time there were no more plays.

Teresa had been officially divorced for a little less than six months after escaping a violent 16year marriage. She had started hustling for more and had even picked up a couple jobs to support her family. Being a single parent with so many children was proving to be a challenge, but she clung to hope. Never had she imagined she would be in this place. Long before that she grew up in a small town in Mexico. Her father had been an affluent member of the community. She was grateful for her childhood and had flourished into a stunning woman. It was not to anyone's surprise when the town's most handsome bachelors came asking for her hand.

Once married, however, his good looks did not help soften the blows from the beatings she began to receive. The first time he beat her, she demanded to be sent home. Then came the calculated accusations, "You're going back home and put that shame on your father? What will people say? You just got married." She stayed.

Initially, the beatings were spread out over time and always followed with gifts, tears, and apologies on bended knees. Then, they began to occur more frequently and more severely. Soon she came to the realization that leaving would no longer be optional if living was to be. She had to go.

Even then, leaving was still a challenging task for Teresa. She had never worked outside the home before, and she only spoke broken English. Despite the abuse, he was the provider.

She remembered back to the night she left and how carefully she had waited for him to fall into his drunken slumber. Quietly she awoke all of her children, and carefully helped them navigate their way through the darkness in whispers. They gathered only what they could carry and piled into the van. There would be no turning back this time. Struggling to see through the pain and swelling from this last beating, Teresa instructed her two oldest sons to push the van into the street before turning on the ignition.

The family van would serve as more than a vehicle in the weeks to come. Initially it was their only shelter, but after a few weeks, she had picked up two jobs—as a waitress and a cook— and they had managed to move into a motel room. It was crowded, but they were safe. And most importantly, they were together.

She saved every penny possible, filed for a restraining order then a divorce. She was exhausted, but they had a roof over their heads and food on the table.

Soon they moved into a home with another family. Hope for a better life was beginning to bear fruit.

Yet, now she stood there, amidst the ashes of her dreams. Disintegrating in that fire were not only their material possessions, but with them the roots of hope that had been growing within her soul.

"Lord, why? Why me? What did I do to deserve this?" were the words crying out from within her soul.

Teresa had tried her best. She prayed. She read her Bible. No matter how hard she tried to be her best she kept taking hits of pain and struggle.

What sin had she committed? What trespasses had she made to warrant this? It wasn't fair.

"God why?" she questioned again as she pulled her kids in around her.

She began to shake uncontrollably. The firemen continued their battle, but Teresa was on the brink of losing hers. *How will I make it to work now? Where will we stay? What will we eat?* Suddenly a loud explosion was heard as her only transportation and what had served as her family's shelter at times, burst into larger ferocious flames.

She cried. Her children cried with her.

As I looked over and saw the woman holding her children, it became clear to me. I remember this moment well. This was a defining moment in our lives, where my mother forfeited the fruit of perseverance. Although she didn't give up the dream for a better life, she gave up her fight for it.

She settled for local jobs bartending, which soon led to an entirely different lifestyle. Sometimes we had food, sometimes we didn't. Sometimes we had running water in our home, sometimes we didn't. Rarely did we have basic necessities for daily living. Memories of my siblings and I, scavenging the local dumpsters for food flooded my mind.

Honestly, I didn't even realize the severity of the dysfunctionality of it all until I had my first child. I was 18 years old and gaining a new revelation of love. For months, I held my newborn daughter closely and I would cry. I cried because of the abuse. I cried because of the neglect. I cried for my family, and I cried for my mother and what it all meant.

<u>Romans 8v28 states:</u>

<u>And we know that all things work together for good to them that love God, to them who are the called according to His purpose.</u>

Even before I completely understood how to "stand on His Promises," God had a plan to take

all these painful events and make them work for my good. Some people in my situation would have held this against their parents. I, however, don't and I never will, in Jesus Name. In fact, instead of holding anger at their failures, I would often use their challenges and defeats to propel past mine.

For example, when I faced a challenge or something difficult like working multiple jobs and countless hours I would refer back to the night of the fire. From this tragedy, I learned that when a parent gives up and metaphorically "loses," it makes it so much harder for their children to "win." I would then ask myself, "Is this it? Is this the battle that's going to knock the fight out of me? If I stop now, where will that leave my children? It was enough to keep me pressing and praying for more."

As I began to walk out different seasons in my life and saw the spiritual principle, found in Romans 8v28, play out, it reinforced my trust in Him.

Everyone encounters painful circumstances, crossroads, and life-altering decisions. Fighting the good fight of faith for a better future is a choice. Nobody can make that decision for you and no human can simply hand over the fruit of perseverance. That is something that must be acquired only through God, sacrifice, and discipline.

Ask yourself: Will you allow the chaotic events in your life to keep you chained down? Or will you keep pressing, in faith, toward your predestined greatness and instead choose to allow the daggers of disappointment, heartache, and even pain that you may experience in life to chisel out the champion within?

One thing is for certain. In this life, we will either reap the fruits or the consequences of our choices. Choose wisely.

I encourage you to choose Jesus.

	Sometimes, people who have not healed completely, look for someone to blame their present circumstances on. In reality, the source of their circumstance is not typically a person. it is their unresolved pain. Often, these people have inner wounds that have not healed, and until they do, there will be a tendency to recycle bad habits and choices in an attempt for the wounds to self-preserve. How can a wound self-preserve?

    Initially we ourselves protect our wounds from others, and in some severe traumatic cases, even from ourselves, but it will be this same coddling of our wounds that will eventually cause the limitations in our lives.

    Envision a person with a broken leg. If this broken bone is not tended to properly, this person will begin to walk in such a way that will prevent putting pressure or causing pain to that leg. Yes, initially, it is that person's choice, but eventually if that leg isn't tended to, it will heal improperly. This improper formation of the bone will eventually cause an abnormal limp. Eventually, the limp will no longer be a choice. There will be no choice left but to adapt to this permanent way of walking, as it is the only way the improperly healed bone will allow. That new gait will eventually limit that person's way of life and affect their quality of it.

The only way to correct the limp is to get to the source of the problem. In the physical realm, the bone must be broken again so that it can be reset properly and then attain proper movement and use of that bone.

How do you reset and heal a heart wound?

First, you have to identify the wound or the issue? Let's use the example of my mother and I. My mother had toxic traits. She could be pretty selfish and self-centered. She could be pretty critical. She didn't call on birthdays. There were no gifts. Not having that relationship hurt growing up. This was my wound.

This wound was comparable to a broken bone, and needed to be set properly. I wanted a relationship with my mother. I needed to heal.

I began to take initiatives towards establishing a healthy relationship. I would call my mother despite how awkward it was. I would go up and hug my mother often and do loving things for my mother, even though I knew it would be a one-way street. In the beginning, my actions of love were not reciprocated. Experiencing the pain of that would be comparable to rebreaking a bone. However, this time I would adopt healthy coping strategies, and these served as aligning a malunion of a bone.

What coping mechanisms? I would take it to God and cry my heart out to Him. After I allowed the Holy Spirit to deal with my emotions and regained my stance on His firm foundation, I would try again.

At times, I would talk to my mom about how her actions affected me. I would talk about our past in a nonjudgmental way and how it affected me. In time, she in return was able to share her perspective and heartache with me.

Through these actions my mother and I developed a new relationship. God was faithful and blessed me by healing that heart wound.

Unfortunately, in some cases, healing a bond directly is not a possibility. Perhaps that person is deceased, or it is not physically or psychologically safe to be around that person. In these cases, healing is still possible.

God is creative. He created the entire universe, and everything in it. Healing is our portion. Healing is His promise to us.

<u>Psalms 147:3.</u>

<u>He heals the brokenhearted and bandages their wounds.</u>

As Jeremiah The Prophet once said, "Nothing is too hard for you." (Jeremiah 32v17)

What I have discovered in this walk is that God often gets creative in healing as well. Healing can come through a wide array of avenues and can look different for everyone. Sometimes, healing heat wounds can include substitute relationships that are rooted in love. Other times, it could be you becoming the person you once needed, and yet still there are times when God allows a supernatural healing that is spontaneous and unexpected. With just one touch God renders all the wounds in our soul healed.

Other times, healing can be a lengthy process. It can include immersing oneself in The Word of God more, as well as counseling, perhaps even a medication for a season.

Jesus once healed by making mud with dirt and his saliva, and even then, there were more steps required for that man to receive his healing.

Healing is not always easy and dealing with inner wounds can be painful, but He has promised to be with us every step of the way, keeping a tab of all our tears. I have had the opportunity to receive different types of healings in different seasons.

Healing often came unexpectedly, even before I realized to the degree in which my soul was bleeding.

Often healing came when I was seeking.

Seeking His Love.

Seeking His Hand.

Seeking to merely understand.

I encourage you to seek Him, and in all your seeking; be healed.

In Jesus Name Amen.

Chapter 4

The Cycle

I continued walking, then, I heard a little girl's voice, and I looked over.

There was a little girl sitting on the edge of a bed, staring, and admiring her mother, as she applied a bright shade of red lipstick onto her full lips. The lipstick matched the red belt that circled her small waist, the red heels she was wearing, and even the cigarette lighter that sat next to her tarot cards. As she slipped the lipstick into her purse, she said a quick prayer, anointed herself with some oil, and headed out.

The little girl watched her as she walked out the front door as did the neighbors sitting out on their porches. Once the car had pulled out of the parking lot of the projects they lived in, the little girl quickly ran over to her mother's makeup and grabbed the brightest shade of lipstick she could find. She faced the mirror and began putting it on.

Then, she heard her little brother begin to cry about being hungry. Her older sister went to the kitchen and put some mustard on a piece of bread and handed it to him.

"I'm so tired of this. She is so selfish. Da**it! There's no food in this house again. There is nothing to eat because your mother likes to forget she has kids," said her sister as her eyes began to water.

I finished crossing and the vision slowly waned away. Memories began to take over my mind and questions began to form. I became discouraged and began to question myself, 'Would my life be the same?'

Then Stacia appeared in a low opacity vision. "You don't have to live in it. Generational curses are meant to be broken. It's never too late, Trust Him," she said.

Right then, I realized that this journey was not just about me. I needed to find my identity so that my children would understand their lineage, and I wanted to break every generational curse that was found within my bloodline.

A little farther down, I looked to my right and there was a street running parallel to my narrow white path. There I saw a little girl sitting on the curb as if she was waiting on someone. She got up from the curb and started walking toward me. I could tell she had been crying. Her clothes were dirty, and her hair was unkempt and tangled. I instantly realized that she was me.

Looking for Jesus

One day, my mom told me about a great man named Jesus who had the power to fix all things. When I asked her where this man could be found, she told me that He could be found at church.

"What church?" I asked.

She said, "Any church."

A few days later and a few streets from my house I saw a building with a cross on it. I excitedly asked my sister, " Is that a church?" She nodded her head.

"Well, when does it open?" I asked.

She replied, "Sunday."

All week, I anxiously waited for Sunday. Every day I asked 'what's today? When is Sunday?' I had a plan to find Jesus. I laid there with my eyes wide open staring up at the ceiling. I didn't know when exactly this building would be open, but I was going to go early. I wouldn't risk missing Him. I smiled to myself and closed my eyes. Visions of my mom smiling and giving me a big hug were prancing around. My mom was going to be so happy once Jesus came and fixed everything. Soon my mom could stay home at night and stop crying all the time. Soon my brothers and sisters would stop fighting and start being a real family. Soon nobody in the house would ever have to run away again.

I just couldn't wait anymore, so I jumped up to get my shoes on to head over to the church. This Jesus sure sounded like a superhero. At that time, I was well-versed with superheroes. I had been sneaking into my brothers' rooms for about two years to look at their comics. I couldn't read the words, but they looked so strong in those pictures. Good guys always won. They would simply take out the bad guys. I just knew Jesus would be my family's superhero.

I quickly got up and walked out of the bedroom. Everyone was still sleeping, and I quietly put my shoes on and slipped out the front door. I looked over, and the flowers were still covered with dew. They always looked so pretty, despite the weeds that surrounded them.

Normally the dark terrified me, but today I didn't care. "Jesus, here I come!" I said as my feet hit the pavement.

I arrived quickly. I could still see the moon. Though it was cold, my excitement provided me with the warmth I needed. Plus, I knew how to stay warm. I shifted from skipping back and forth to standing next to a wall huddled in a ball to conserve heat. None of that mattered though. I was focused on all of the things I would ask Jesus for, food, clothes, coins for the laundromat, and of course, toys! I smiled.

As the time passed, the moon quietly slipped away, and the sun to begin to make its grand entrance or the day but the church remained quiet. The birds were chirping, the streets were beginning to yawn but nobody had opened the doors yet, and I began to get worried that maybe I had already missed Him. Maybe I got the wrong day. I got up and started pacing in front of the church. My concern was steadily growing.

Then finally a car pulled up. Alarmed, they let me in and led me into the kitchen. After pouring me a glass of milk and giving me some cookies, they began to question me. "Where are your parents? Are you OK? How long have you been sitting here?" they asked.

I reassured them that I was OK and then explained that I was here for Jesus. When they were assured of my safety, they ushered me into a back row in the sanctuary where I waited until church started. As people began to enter the building, I would catch them staring at me. I did not have proper Sunday school hygiene or attire. I didn't own a toothbrush. There was rarely any toothpaste in my home. I had no hairbrush. The clothes I wore, I had been wearing over and over for days, and I hadn't bathed all week. I sat there with people sneering at me with looks of disgust.

Honestly, I was extremely uncomfortable, but I wasn't there for them. I was there for Jesus.

Shortly after, I followed a group of children into a classroom where nobody really talked to me. Suddenly I decided I had had enough and asked the Sunday school teacher for Jesus. That's when she dropped the 'truth.' She told me that we could only learn about Him at church and that Jesus was not a real person anymore. I held back tears as I listened.

As I walked home that day, I was filled with disappointment. I felt hopeless. Not only did I not see Jesus in a physical sense, but looking back, the "church" appeared to lack the concept of Jesus in spirit, and after that it would be a few years before I tried church again.

Yet still, I am grateful for experiencing life in that way and to have had people judge me at such an early age. That experience taught me one of the most important lessons of my life. It was that day I promised myself that I would never judge anyone based on what they looked like or how they were dressed. I learned that day the importance of looking beyond a person's exterior, be it physically or characteristically.

I continued to walk past that scene. I was trying to shake off the memories. Stacia said to not think about the past, but it was all I could see.

"Tough, huh?" I heard, I stopped a moment and pulled out the mask.

"Nobody said this was going to be easy, but it will be worth it. You just gotta get some stick-to-it-iveness, and before you know it, you will be there. It could be a lot worse. You have to stay grateful for where you are right now. It's a process, but you can do it," said Doc.

Suddenly, I could also feel someone looking at me, but I couldn't see anything.

Then Doc said, "You feel that? That's your inner man, also known as your Spirit, telling you something is coming near. You have to learn to listen to that."

"But I don't see anything," I replied, looking around again.

"When are you going to get it, young lady?" Doc asked, smacking his teeth. "Let me show you," he continued.

As I placed the mask over my eyes, I could see that suddenly there was more darkness than light around me, and it appeared my angels were being outnumbered as the battle ensued all around me.

Then I heard Doc say, "You got to pray in The Spirit; Do it now!"

I began to pray in the Spirit, and as I prayed the skies opened and more angels descended from above. Not just that, but the angels who appeared to be losing began to gain strength and defeated their shadow-like opponents.

"Just like that. When you feel that and when your emotions change or something doesn't feel right, you pray just like that," said Doc.

Just then a fireball flew past my face. I carefully pulled the mask away and placed it back in the bag. I sighed as the dark atmosphere was converted back to the previous colorful scenery. I began to walk again when I noticed a sign ahead that read "1980s".

The '80s represented my childhood—a very crucial stage in life. The first five years in life are vital and actually are known to have a huge impact on developing our adult personality, because of this children should be brought up in stable, consistent, and loving homes. Unfortunately, for some this has not been the case, and instead they have been forced to walk, sleep, and eat chaos and calamity on a daily basis.

During this time, traits and mindsets of a victim, survivor, or that of a victor will begin to develop and follow the child into adulthood.

Being "dysfunctional" would be a step up from what my childhood consisted of. While other kids drank Kool-Aid and fought with their parents about taking a bath, I often had to figure out which neighbor's faucet I would use to fill my bucket to flush our commode. To paint a clearer picture, it wasn't just the lack of material possessions—honestly, I grew up in the projects. I knew lots of families who were 'going through' just like us. The difference, however, is that there was still love in their home. Our home was lacking everything. There was no obvious or intentional love, no kindness, and no unity. In my family, people were very mean and purposely vicious to one another.

My mother thought she had escaped that life, but in actuality, an abusive spirit had trickled down from one sibling to the next in a domino effect. Violence erupted in my household on a daily basis. It was an 'every man for himself' mentality, where the weak man was severely punished for being weak. Everyone was always yelling, fighting and/or putting each other down. Being one of the youngest, I quickly learned not to make people mad. In fact, if anyone was ever nice to me, I made sure to try to keep them happy at whatever cost to myself. If I ever just so happened to make someone mad, I would apologize for days at a time—anything to keep them happy.

Soon, I lost my voice and my ability to make decisions that could potentially go against someone else's. As time passed, I learned how to be tough physically to cover up for my internal insecurities and weaknesses.

I took a big sigh and just felt so grateful for everything God had done in my life and the different ways that He had liberated me.

The road seemed to go on and on. Then I saw a sign that read, "Abuse Untold."

I knew what this street was all about.

Abuse Untold

I was sexually abused for the first time at the age of 4. Unfortunately, with my older siblings in school, it often left my younger brother and me to fend for ourselves. Often, we would find ourselves in the homes of different people. One of these places was the home of an elderly couple.

I began to pray in the Spirit as I took a deep breath, and the memories came flooding back.

I remembered the man calling me over to him. Something didn't feel right, but I didn't want to make him mad at me, reluctantly, I walked closer to him. He grabbed me and sat me on top of his lap, and I could hear his belt buckle loosen. He quickly pushed my panties to the side with one hand, and I could feel him on me. "You like it right?" He whispered in my ear as he began moving me on him, back and forth. He was breathing heavily.

My heart was racing. I was terrified and though my eyes were tearing up, I made myself smile because I did not want to make him mad at me. "Do you like it?" He asked me as he continued to stimulate me, I sat there in terror and shock, not understanding and not knowing what to do.

Then suddenly his wife came out the back door calling us in for lunch, and he immediately stopped. He hugged me closely and said, "Don't tell anyone or they'll put me in jail." He kissed my cheek as he let me down.

Terrified, I ran to the outhouse in their backyard and locked myself in. I was trembling and crying. Though I was only 4, I knew something wasn't right, but I didn't understand what or how to explain it.

Suddenly, he was at the door trying to force it open. I could see him through the crack of the door; he was staring in at me. "Little girl, open the door. Open the door!" he said. I sat there frozen in fear, and I could not move.

I finished crossing the street as the vision disappeared. My body was shaking, and I inhaled the fresh air deeply. I have no memory of what happened the rest of that day. What I do remember is crying and screaming whenever my mother attempted to take us back. I also remember multiple visits to the doctor for different infections.

I would like to say that this was an isolated occurrence, but unfortunately more incidents would occur throughout my childhood and young teen years in the homes of people who were "looking after" me.

After those experiences, no matter how much I bathed, I always felt dirty. As I got older, I accepted toxic situations because after all, who was I to expect anything better? I was so acclimated to toxic relationships and environments that even when I finally had a legit idea of what healthy was, there was no way I could feel worthy enough of one for myself. Yet against all odds, here I was resolved to have better. If not for myself, then the motivation of claiming such a life for my children kicked in.

Memories of events with my children began to kick in. Mistakes I had made, poor decisions. "I have been redeemed," I said out loud.

As I got older and was entrusted with my children and their safety. I found myself in the midst of a whole new level of warfare and one that had it not been the constant intervention of The Holy Spirit could have been so much worse.

My heart cringes at studies that show the high percentage of sexual abuse. Childhood experiences matter; all of them. Children's emotions are very pure and because they are untrained, they are very honest. How are they reacting when certain adults or other kids come around? Pay attention to who you leave your children with, family or not.

It was the one closest to Jesus who betrayed him. No matter what your financial situation, you should never be too busy to pray for your children and then take time to listen to The Holy Spirit. You believe your child is anointed; you say? Guard them even more. Trust that even in the fetal stage there is a target out on them already. Listen to them. Never believe that someone else knows better than you when it comes to their discipline and love. It was you and your love that was entrusted with His Rod and His Staff. That soul was entrusted to your hands. Yes, you can take counsel. Yes, go to therapy, but always trust *your* love. Trust your gut. Trust His Love and the fact that God has you.

Suddenly, I began to feel fear again, and I started praying. I put the mask on and could see my angels were fighting for me. On the sidelines, I saw multiple dark shadows headed towards me and gaining ground fast. I started to run in fear. I looked back, and one of my angels flew down and struck it down with his sword.

In a panic, I stopped and snatched the mask off my face. When I turned around, the scenery had returned to its cheerful state. I slowed down to catch my breath. I looked down at the mask and tried catching my breath. Doc said, "You must get stronger. Use your faith. It's going to be all right. Keep walking. Keep pressing."

Then, a fiery arrow flew past us, interrupting him mid-speech. He continued, saying, "And PLEASE be careful," as he rolled his eyes, ``I can't afford another crack."

I quickly but carefully put him back in my bag.

"God bless America. I don't know if I can do this," I whispered to myself as I turned to face the road.

"Young lady, watch your words. They have power," I heard Doc say from the bag. "Of course, you can do this, without a doubt, but you must be more careful with your words.

The beginning of <u>*Isaiah 55v11 says:*</u>

<u>*'So shall my word be that goes out from my mouth; it shall not return to me empty, but shall accomplish that which I purpose, and shall succeed in the thing for which I sent it.'*</u>

In short, young lady if you think you can, you can! But if you speak you can't, then you can't!"

I knew Doc was right but saying that was so much easier to say than to actually do. Especially when your mind isn't trained to think the best. I continued to walk and reflected to my elementary years. I had mixed feelings about school growing up.

Although I loved reading and being involved, I had a challenging time adjusting. Often, I didn't fit in, and it wasn't just the students. It was the teachers as well.

Teachers have the power to assist in the building up or in the breaking down of a student. Often if a child is having a rough time at home, school can become a safe haven. For me, however, that was not the case.

As I continued on the white path, I approached another crossroad. I looked up and saw a gray sign that read "Elementary Essentials."

Suddenly, I heard a school bell, and I took my first step.

Elementary Essentials

Suddenly, I saw several children lying on mats, except for one little girl who was lying on a towel. I could see two teachers sitting down having lunch at their desks, and I could hear one saying to the other, "She is just not clean, and that's gross." She laid there pretending to be asleep and keeping her eyes closed.

"She's just nasty, and her mom never shows up to parent-teacher conferences. I can only imagine what she's like," said one teacher.

I heard the little girl sniffle, and then I heard the teacher say, "G.G., are you awake? You are supposed to be sleeping. Close your eyes and sleep. Oh yes, and remind me to paddle you after nap time for not following directions."

The little girl quickly turned and closed her eyes. A short time later, they were getting ready for snack time when the teacher said, "G.G. I haven't forgotten. Please come to the front of the classroom."

The little girl slowly walked up to the front and the teacher went to her cabinet and pulled out the paddle as the entire classroom watched.

I was in kindergarten, and this teacher did not like me. In fact, she took every opportunity she could to paddle me and humiliate me in front of the class. I was only 5 and hadn't yet learned how to stand up for myself. I didn't understand that teachers or adults could be wrong. I accepted everything she told me about myself as facts.

My eyes watered and I stood dead in my tracks, unable to advance any farther in crossing the street. Between home and school, by the time I had entered the 2nd grade, my self-esteem was depleted.

I looked down at my pink Nikes and thought to myself, "I can't do it. What's the point?" I mumbled softly as tears began to stream down my face.

Then suddenly I heard a little girl crying to my right, so I looked up and despite the tears burning in my eyes, I saw another vision.

I was 8 years old, sitting in front of my 2nd grade teacher, Mrs. Glass. I sat there crying to her. I was apologizing. The red-headed older woman looked at me, readjusted her glasses and asked, "Why are you crying, G.G.?"

"Because, Mrs. Glass, I'm dirty and I'm gross," I cried.

The teacher looked at me and said, "So change it."

"How? How am I supposed to do that?" I cried.

"Take a bath at night," she said.

"My mom hides the soap. She puts it in her room because she says us kids waste it. We have no clothes, and the clothes we do have are dirty," I replied.

Mrs. Glass looked at me and spoke sternly.

"Now you listen to me, GG. You stop feeling sorry for yourself. If your mother doesn't wash your clothes, wash your own clothes. Put them in the water, put soap in there and scrub. When I was little I only had two dresses, and I had to wash my own clothes every day after school. If I can do it, you can do it.

"You choose who you are going to be, G.G.. If you don't want to be dirty, take a bath. If you want clean clothes, wash them. You are a smart girl, and you have a brilliant future ahead of you. Stop wasting time, feeling sorry for yourself and think of ways to help yourself," said Mrs. Glass.

I stood there, halfway through this road. I was thinking about Mrs. Edna J. Glass, one of the kindest people I had ever met up to that point in my life.

The school bell got louder. I looked over to my left again, and I saw Mrs. Glass bringing me a dress. She had bought it for me for the weekend's talent and arts competition.

I was so excited about this dress; it was pretty and blue. It was a relief when I unbuttoned my jeans and released the pressure on my belly from them being so tight. I quickly kicked them off, rubbed my hand over the deep imprint they left and wiped off a tinge of blood where the pants had actually cut into my skin.

I looked over at my pretty dress and picked it up. Beneath the dress, I noticed she even got me a new clean pair of panties and nylons. I quickly put on everything, and shortly after, Mrs. Glass knocked on the door.

"Can I come in?" she asked.

"Yes ma'am," I responded.

She came in and brushed my hair out of my face and pinned it back in barrettes.

"Ok, G.G., let's practice one more time, but in front of the class this time," she said.

As I stepped out, all of my classmates' mouths dropped open at my transformation. I smiled with a big grin and began to recite.

I was filled with a feeling of gratitude at this point. Mrs. Glass was able to relate to me, and I developed a level of trust with her. She helped me to get involved in poetry slams, which changed everything for me. I started participating in plays and recitals, which I received many awards for. I had finally found something I was good at, and the joy I obtained from it, helped me to offset the conditions at home.

Mrs. Glass's influence and impact was such a pivotal point in my life. She inspired me and gave me the gift of hope.

For you teachers out there, don't lose your shine. For many students, you are the only light they have to help lead them out of the darkness. Keep your light burning bright.

The Dress

The figures began to fade away. With a smile on my face, I whispered, "Thank you, Mrs. Edna J. Glass, for your kindness to me."

I had almost finished crossing over the road when the next vision hit me with the speed of lightning.

The school bell stopped ringing, and I heard Madonna's song, "Like a Prayer," playing in the background. There was an older girl singing on the stage. Although this girl had been performing for years, she had a summer off. She had taken her talent for granted. Mrs. Glass had retired, and she did not have a coach. She had not been practicing, and she was not prepared. The entire school was watching, and in the midst of her routine, she froze. She had forgotten her dance moves, and she swiftly jolted off stage.

That was the last time I performed. For a while I had found a way out, and then just like that, it was gone. The fear of failure had now been added to a growing list of barriers I would have to overcome if I was ever going to reach my destiny. I took my last step off that road and continued on my path, thinking of these bittersweet memories.

For now, I was happy to take another step. Every step was one step closer to Mr. El and I continued my journey.

Chapter 5

Intersections and Detours

A strategy the enemy often uses is to take an experience and play it over and over and over until it has been deeply embedded in your mind. Then it becomes a stronghold in your mindset and dictates how you react in any given moment and in any given circumstance. It can remain a constant battle for the person until they learn how to reprogram and guard their thought life.

<u>Mark 2 v22 says this:</u>

<u>"And no one puts new wine into old wineskins; or else the new wine bursts the wineskins, the wine is spilled, and the wineskins are ruined. But new wine must be put in new wineskins."</u>

I used to have this stethoscope. I used it for so long that eventually the rubber it was made of lost its elasticity and became stiff, and lost its ability to bend, eventually it broke. This is the same concept. New ways of thinking and new standards of living cannot be achieved by old ways of thinking and thought patterns. How do you get new wineskins of the mind?

There are steps to acquiring new wineskins of the mind. The first step is to expose the current state of mind to The Word of God.

Why? This is comparable to dropping colored paint on an ultra-white sheet. Even the smallest drop of color is obvious to the naked eye. In a similar way, exposure to The Truth exposes erroneous belief systems, thought processes, and bad habits. Once it is exposed, the second step is more likely to occur.

The second step is to acknowledge the toxicity of the "old way" aka the old wineskins of our minds. Some of these mindsets and behaviors, that were initially created to protect our hurts, have developed into strongholds that the enemy uses to limit us and keep us confined to less than who we were created to be. Yet, be encouraged, for it is only a matter of time before even the most fortified of these strongholds is exposed and The Holy Spirit begins to break through and set us free. Again, it will take time and consistent exposure to The Living Word of God for these strongholds to be identified, but once we have acknowledged their existence, we can continue to step 3.

The third step will be to replace the old mindset with the new mindset. This new mindset will be our new wineskin. The new wineskin in our minds will allow us to hold a better vision for ourselves and what is attainable. Once we see a clearer or a more beautiful vision of ourselves, for ourselves it then becomes easier to release those bad habits and thought processes and replace them with better choices and habits.

When this happens, the fruits of this change will be evident in our lives by healthier environments, relationships, and overall increase. Again, some behaviors will be easier to change, but others will need constant correction and may only change gradually over time.

As minutes passed, I was even more anxious to meet Mr. El. I had so many questions that tied into one big question, which had everything to do with my identity. How do I break past these obstacles and break free from these curses? What does an identity in Christ look like? And am I really qualified to receive that?

I looked over at a street full of weeds and bushes and began to feel uneasy again with every step I took. Yet despite the fear I felt, I just kept praying and moving ahead because I knew that my answer was somewhere on this white narrow road.

Suddenly, I noticed that the white road was duplicated. They intertwined, so I wasn't sure which way to go. I heard a voice say, "It's the one on the right." I looked around, but I didn't see anyone.

Then I noticed that down on my right side behind a tall green tree, there was a woman with a bright pink bandana sitting on a bench. I slowly walked over to her.

"Don't worry, I won't bite," she said. She was wrapped up in a blanket with a piece of paper in her hand. I reached out my hand.

"Hello, my name is G.G.," I said.

"Hello, my name is Fanci. I've never seen you around. What brings you here?" she asked.

I told her about my plans to see Mr. El.

"Well, I was on a journey too. I was supposed to see someone named Jehovah-Rapha. I just got tired and quit," she said.

She looked down and handed me a piece of paper. It was a report with big black letters spelling out CANCER.

I stood there silently, carefully trying to find the words to say.

"I am so sorry." I said as I stood there in more silence, and after a few more moments I spoke again.

"Hey Fanci, but I don't know a Jehovah Rapha but I am sure Mr. El can help anyways. I have only heard great things about him."

"I used to believe that, but now I am so confused. I thought I was so close, and I just can't believe that this is happening to me. I got caught up in thinking about how terribly this is going to affect me and my children. I just don't know what I'm going to do," cried Fanci.

"One day I was leaving the hospital after chemotherapy, and it just happened to be raining. I was so upset and crying that I lost focus. My car spun off the road and ended up here. I was told to follow the white narrow road, but my emotions overwhelmed me, so I decided to sit down, then I just never got back up," she said.

"Well, Fanci, I really don't want to take this journey alone. Come with me. Maybe as we walk, we can find out more about each other and get there faster," I said.

Fanci laid back and closed her eyes for a moment as in deep thought.

"Yes." Fanci said as she stood up, stretched, and began folding up her bright yellow blanket, "Let's go."

We were getting to know each other when suddenly we came across our next road, and it had a huge sign that read "Bed of Tears." Fanci stopped dead in her tracks.

"Fanci, are you OK?" I asked, but I knew the expression on her face all too well.

"G.G., I can't," Fanci's voice became shaky. Her eyes filled up with tears as she shook her head from side to side, crying, "No."

Then Doc spoke up, "Fanci, you are strong. You can do this."

Fanci looked shocked as she looked around. "Who said that?" she asked.

I looked down at my bag and pulled out Doc.

"I did. You just need to have faith and be of good courage. God is with you," said Doc.

"Fanci, meet Doc. He's been my guide here," I said.

"Fanci, Mr. El can help you, but you must keep moving no matter how you feel or what it looks like. You are not alone," Doc continued.

Fanci received words of encouragement.

"Now, let's continue on ladies," he said.

I placed the mask back into safety, and I curled my arm around Fanci's. We took a deep breath and slowly placed our feet on the dark cracked street.

Bed of Tears

The woman laid on the bed. She had just had a mastectomy. She was hurting everywhere. She didn't understand how this could happen to her. She was an active church member and paid her tithes and offerings. Yet here she was, too weak to get out of bed on her own, and chemotherapy was to start on Monday. She reached down to the gauze dressing on her chest. *How will my husband look at me now?* she thought. As she reached for her phone, her arm brushed the top of the pillow, which was soaking wet from her tears.

"Lord, give me strength," she cried quietly.

Then suddenly she heard her husband come in the front door with their children. She heard his footsteps approach their bedroom door, and then it gently opened.

He came in, sat down next to her, and gently held her hand, "How are you doing baby?" "I'm OK," said Fanci.

Her eyes watered. They didn't need this right now. Their relationship had already been strained.

"Hey Fanci, I know this isn't the best timing, but we have to talk," her husband said.

At that point, Fanci had been trying to sit herself up very carefully, so as not to bust open any of the stitches. She locked eyes with him.

"Yes?" she asked.

"I won't be coming home tonight... or anymore. I'm sorry to do this right now but I'm moving out. Fanci. I will always be here for the kids" he spoke slowly as he lowered his eyes.

Fanci froze in her path.

"It's OK. You're not alone." I said.

I handed her some tissue from my pocket. I nudged her forward a little. She took another step.

"This is hard, G.G.," Fanci said.

"Who are you telling? God Bless America," I replied, as I placed my hand on my forehead.

Together, in silence, we focused on crossing over and jumped right back onto the narrow white road.

"This path is not for the faint of heart, but my mama didn't raise no punk," she took a deep breath, while tightening up her hankie, "You know you are right on something. It's definitely easier when you aren't alone," she said with a smile.

"Iron sharpens iron," Doc chimed in.

"And remember what the Bible says about when two are gathered. These are spiritual principles ladies. You are constantly engaged in spiritual warfare, whether you are able to see it yet or not. This is why you must start reading this
Bible for yourselves." He continued,

"Matthew 18v20 states: "For where two or three are gathered together in my name, there am I in the midst of them.'

God is with you, and if God is for you ladies," Doc continued, "Who can be against you?"

Then, suddenly we started to sense something very strange. It grew darker. I looked up and saw a dark cloud.

"What is going on?" I asked.

"I don't know. I've been here for a while, and I have never seen this before," said Fanci.

Then Doc said, "You are starting to see The Truth with your own eyes. Don't be scared. No matter what happens, trust God and just keep going."

There was so much going through my mind at this point. I had begun to get even more anxious to find Mr. El as we continued to walk. I began to pray in the Spirit.

Then, a vision of a woman walking toward us holding a baby appeared. I gently smiled and began to wave at her, but as the woman passed us by, I realized she bore no face. I stopped and turned as I watched the woman walk into what appeared to be a dark abandoned building. I then looked at the name of the street. It was called "Life Snatchers."

"Aww, man. Could we have rested a little more before we hit another one?" said Fanci as she threw her hands in the air.

We looked at each other and took the first step together.

Vision of Lies

The lady sat there rocking back and forth, staring at the stones lying on the table in the dimmed room. She looked at the gray stones as if she was watching a movie, and she quietly grinned. Each stone had its own unique individual marking.

Life Snatchers

Though I had grown up in a family that frequented psychics, and some who had the ability to read tarot cards, I had never sat in front of a psychic for my own dealings. However, at this moment, I was in extreme desperation and felt I had nowhere to turn. I needed some direction in my life and decided to try the place with the neon "Fortune Teller" sign.

As I sat there awaiting some answers, the lady began rocking back and forth more intensely and giggling loudly to herself. I didn't know what to make of it, and I was quickly beginning to regret my decision. Then suddenly, she brushed a gray strand of hair behind her right ear and said, "You know you don't have to have it if you don't want to. You're so young, and you have your whole life ahead of you."

My eyebrows raised as she began to explain. "It's called an affirmation. All you have to do is tell the world that you are not ready to have this baby, and you won't. Every time you think about it or start to get worried, just say, "World, I am not ready to have this baby," she said.

Quickly I asked, "Really? That's it?"

She said "Yes."

As odd and eerie as this woman was, as soon as I left her presence, I immediately began to recite the words that she had said to me: "World, I am not ready to have this baby."

This was a simple solution, or so I thought. I was 18 years old and had just been accepted into Michigan State University on a summer scholarship. I was scheduled to move into the dorms the day after I graduated so that I could begin my first semester as a freshman in pre-law majoring in International Affairs. This pregnancy was unintended and was interfering with my plans.

I repeated those words often: first thing in the morning, on my way to the bus stop and all day and night, repeatedly, walking down the school hallways, I said this phrase. I would be washing dishes and would continue repeating these words again. I would repeat them yet again before I went to sleep. If there was a way out of the situation, I was going to take it.

Three days later, I began to show signs of a miscarriage and had to rush to the emergency room. After different diagnostics were performed, the doctor walked in and said, "There's nothing else we can do. You can stay here and be monitored, or you can go home so your body can complete the miscarriage In the comfort of your home. I'll give you a moment to think about it." Then he stepped out.

As I lay there on the hospital bed, I began to cry. I felt guilt, shame, and remorse. Had my words really caused this? I hadn't been to church since I was a young child, but right then and there, I did the only thing I knew how to do.

I immediately asked God for forgiveness, and I apologized for releasing those words out of my mouth. I asked Him to please take care of my baby and to help me. I really did not know what to do or who to turn to. As soon as I left the hospital that day, I did the only thing I knew how to do. If my words had caused this, then maybe my words could undo this. I also decided to include Jesus in my prayers.

That day I began to say repeatedly and fervently, "Lord, thank you for my healthy baby. Thank you that my child has life. Thank you that my child is born healthy. Lord, I thank you for my baby."

For the next three days I repeated my thanksgiving, and I thanked God profusely for my healthy baby every opportunity I got. On the third day, the bleeding stopped, but my words declaring health and life over my baby did not.

A few months later, on Halloween night, not only did I give birth to my beautiful daughter, but I had unknowingly claimed victory in my first spiritual battle. This experience taught me the power of my words.

As I continued to watch the scene play out, the lady entered the office and handed them her money and her baby. Then the door closed, and audible screams could be heard.

More black figures started heading toward us. Angry women with raven black hair were rushing in our direction holding up butcher knives.

"Fanci, I'm scared," I said.

"What is it?" asked Fanci.

"Don't you see those women running toward us?" I said.

"I don't see any women," she replied.

"Run, Fanci, run," I said as I started.

Fanci yelled, "G.G., what's wrong?"

As she started running with me, I looked down and realized I had dropped my bag a few yards back.

Fanci, I dropped my bag," I yelled.

"Whaaaaaat?!" yelled Fanci.

We both came to an abrupt stop and turned around. The women giving chase were gone, but so was my bag.

"My bag is gone. Where is it? Fanci! We can't do this without Doc. I can't do this without Doc!" I shouted, feeling frustrated, whaling my arms in the air, searching frantically everywhere. My heart was pounding so loudly that I was sure Fanci could hear it.

"G.G.!" Fanci interrupted. Doc told us to have faith and to just keep going no matter what. We gotta keep moving forward." she said.

I continued to search, "we can't leave him like that Fanci! This isn't right. He is the one who knows this land.``

"G.G." Fanci said firmly.

Hesitantly, I stopped a moment and placed both hands on my forehead, and looked down at the ground. Inhaling briskly and inhaling slowly my world stopped spinning and my heart beat calmed down. I nodded my head in agreement, turned around and started walking forward. I didn't know if I was ready yet to go on without Doc, but I didn't have another choice. I hoped our time together had prepared me for what we were dealing with and for anything headed our way.

Filled with doubt, we continued on our journey.

Chapter 6
The Climb

I hadn't had anything to eat and suddenly felt the weariness in my body.

"I'm getting hungry," said Fanci.

"Yeah me too, but we can't deviate from this path. Let's keep pushing."

It was definitely getting dark, and we would have to find somewhere to rest soon. Doc had already warned us that this journey would become more dangerous in the absence of light.

I could almost hear Doc telling me 'no matter what it looks like, you gotta' have Faith.' Faith! Do you know what faith is, young lady?" Doc had asked once.

"Faith is the substance of things hoped for, but the evidence of things not seen. Without hope there can be no faith." I realized then that losing Doc had momentarily knocked the hope out of me. I started reminding myself of why I started this journey. I envisioned my family and the innate way I had been equipped with a spirit that refused to settle. Surely, we did not get this far to only make it this far. There had to be more. It could not end this way. Soon we were able to see the top of the hill we were on. Suddenly I became hopeful that once we reached the top of the hill, we would have a better view of the land and a better idea of what to do next.

"I know Mr. El will have answers for us, Fanci," I added, "and I just know that once we reach the top of this hill, something great is going to happen."

"You are so right!" yelled Fanci. "G.G, let's do this. Despite the way we feel, let's just push ourselves even more and run the rest of the way up!"

Then we started sprinting up the hill and suddenly felt a surge of energy flowing through us. As we continued to run, we began hearing strange noises, and things began to move in the dimmed lighting of the evening all around us, which inspired us to run faster. Just as we reached the top of a hill, the moon made its entrance. With its light, we saw its reflection on what seemed like a purple house. "Fanci, is that a purple house?" I looked over. "...and a purple car!" said Fanci, "And it's smack dab in the middle of the narrow white road!! Let's go!"

We raced to the bottom of the hill. And as we came to the front of the house, we saw someone swinging on a hammock.

"What are y'all doing out here at this time of night?" A blonde-haired lady stood up off the swing with the widest brightest smile. Before we could answer she opened her door and said,

"Come on in, y'all must be starving. My name is Mary Sonshine Holder Of Light. My friends call me MJ or Sonshine." She had the most beautiful blue eyes that had a unique twinkle that you could see even in the dark. Her essence emitted a sense of love and warmth that instantly gave us a sense of security.

"Hi, I'm G.G, and this is Fanci. Thank you so much for letting us in!" I said.

By now it was really dark out there.

"Certainly, you guys must be exhausted! You know I had my doubts about the location of this place when Mr. El instructed me to build here, but it turns out he really knew what he was doing! Sometimes I take a walk out there and it's so sad to see the people who gave up while going up the hill. Sometimes I even walk to the top of the hill and look out for the weary. Sometimes I can get to them in time to encourage them, But even so, not everyone makes it," Mary said while looking down, then looked back at us. "If they had pushed just a little further, a little longer, then they would find me. Mr. El placed me here to show love and kindness and help replenish you with any supplies and rest so you can continue your journey," she said, as she opened her door. "Come on inside, girls."

That night, we spoke of our journey, about Doc but also feasted, like royalty, amidst the most colorful spread of the finest delicacies ever. Then we rested. The next morning, MJ gave us fresh clothes and handed us new bags with fruits to sustain us for the rest of our journey. As we took a few steps, I looked back and saw her eyes twinkling once more. She smiled and I knew she had been placed there as a

reservoir of hope for the lost. I took a moment and just gave God thanks. Then, I whispered, "Thank you Mary
Sonshine."

Soon enough, we came upon our next crossroad and the sign read, "And Your Little Children Too." As our feet hit the pavement, the next vision came.

Your Little Children, Too

My brother repeatedly kept slamming my head on the wall. "Now what, G.G.? Say something now!" he continued to yell at me as speckles of spit were landing on my face.

All I could do was cry as he continued to drag me by my hair to the next wall. There was no help. There was no intervention. This was my life.

For many years, the abuse remained dormant in my soul, and I learned to use anger as a weapon. During the times I felt threatened or intimidated I would simply draw from it, like a magic potion or pill, it would allow me to transform myself into this powerful being.

But as with any drug, you think you are in control until one day you realize that it actually controls you.

And so, it was with me. I didn't think it was a problem until I had my own children. It was not until then that I realized that every time I said yes and partook of anger, that it rooted deeper within my heart.

I began to reflect. There was a time when my children received more chastisement and spankings than love.

The visions continued;

I was in the house with my children. As I looked out the front door, I saw this woman with wild red hair rushing towards us. She was waving a butcher knife in her hand.

She had every means of coming in and destroying my children. I knew I would have to battle her to keep them safe. I called out to their Nana and asked her to protect them while I dealt with this evil. As she closed herself off into a room with the children, I prepared to head out. I stepped out the front door of my house ready to go to battle for these children of mine.

The woman came, angrily swinging her knife, but I held my ground and battled. I hit her with all my might. It was a ferocious fight. I continued to land blow after blow until I finally had her pinned to the ground. When I looked down at her face, she began to laugh and said, "I am you."

As we passed that vision and continued on our journey again, I realized that the vision had been previously given to me in a dream once when God began correcting my heart and my hand towards my children.

He showed me through this dream that I was hurting my children. I quickly repented and began dealing with the seeds of anger and physical abuse planted deep within my heart. I began reading books to gain an understanding, and I prayed for God to keep my children safe, even from me. I paid close attention to the Word at church. More than anything, I asked God to eradicate anything in my heart that could hurt my children. I loved them, and they deserved the best from me.

"Thank you, Lord,"

As we hit the narrow white road again, the next sign quickly introduced itself.

It read, "The Cards Don't Lie" and had a picture of tarot cards underneath it. Then an old man in a black robe approached us.

"You both look lost. Maybe I can be of some help," he said.

But something didn't sit right with me about him. I quietly prayed in the Spirit.

"We are on our way to see Mr. El," said Fanci.

"Mr. El? That's why you're lost. There is no Mr. El. He doesn't exist. You should be going to see Mr. S.," said the guy.

"That is not what we were told," I said.

"Let me guess." He rolled his eyes. "You met Stacia, and she told you to follow the narrow white road. SMH," he threw up both arms in a questioning manner, "Ladies listen. I'm gonna look out for yall and I'm gonna tell you the truth. What you want to do is follow the wide, cracked black road. Sure, it looks a little ragged but that's only because people use it so much. It's really a shortcut. It's kinda like taking the alley. There are so many people on it, which means it's the right way," he said.

"Well, how do we get there?" asked Fanci.

"Let's see what the cards say," he said as he brought out a stack of tarot cards.

"No, we don't need your help!" I shouted as I grabbed Fanci's elbow.

We started walking away quickly.

"You're making a big mistake!" he yelled at us.

Then his countenance darkened, and he followed us yelling, "We already got your little mask friend, and we are coming for both of you!"

Just as I turned around, he did a 360 and disappeared into thin air.

"We will get Doc back. We gotta stay focused and follow the path. Stacia said there would be opposition. We just have to stay on this white road," I said.

This street brought back a lot of memories. Often my mother would just sit on the couch with a cigarette in one hand and tarot cards in the other. This was a normal activity in our house. Not understanding the seriousness of it, sometimes after she'd gone to work, if we needed money for food, I would sometimes grab my mother's tarot cards and go from apartment to apartment, pretending to know what I was doing and charging people to do so. Though for me it was only a way to make money, the power of those cards over my family was very real. We were raised to have so much faith in those cards.

"G.G. do not freak out, but we do gotta cross this street too. Come on girl. Let's do this," said Fanci as she tapped me on my shoulder.

The Cards Don't Lie

I was 11. years old. I was standing at a bus stop, and an older high school girl came and pushed me. I was afraid.

Finally, after a couple weeks of bullied, I went to my older sister Teri, and confided in her. Furious, she demanded to know who the girl was.

"Who is she? Why are you letting her pick on you? You better go to school tomorrow and whoop her tail," she said.

"I can't. I'm scared, I'm a 7th grader and she's in high school!" I cried.

"G.G. don't be stupid, come here," my sister said, pulling out my mom's tarot cards.

"I see here that if you go and confront her, you're gonna win," she said.

I started laughing, but my sister was serious. She reminded me that the cards don't lie. I believed her.

I woke up the next morning, pumped up and full of courage. I was so confident that the cards were on point. I rushed to the bus stop, assured of my victory, walked right up to the girl, and threw down my books.

"Come on. You want to fight. Let's go!" I said.

My bully backed down, and my faith in those cards grew.

Habakkuk 2:18 (ESV)

"What profit is an idol when its maker has shaped it, a metal image, a teacher of lies? For its maker trusts in his own creation when he makes speechless idols!"

Tarot cards, horoscopes, and other new age items are linked to a supernatural entity, but that spiritual link is not of God. Sadly, many people have no idea who they are, nor of their purpose and find themselves anxiously seeking guidance, and many times unknowingly submit to the authority of the demon linked to the psychic or item. That's right. They may get a little bit of facts revealed to them but have also formed a demonic pact or covenant. This covenant unknowingly grants access to their souls and their homes. Suddenly, the person who accepted that reading may find they don't understand and can't believe their "bad luck."

Such was my life. Restless, anxious, and directionless. Horoscopes and psychics were the only guidance I had in my life and the only guidance my rebellious spirit would allow me to submit to. I was 16 years old and renting a room from a friend. I was working a couple of jobs, trying to finish school and had no idea what to do.

I would purchase the monthly horoscopes with daily readings and read them over and over again looking for these readings to come to pass. Expecting it to come to pass, sometimes, even subconsciously aligning my actions and choices to make these things come to pass. I knew of God and yeah of course I said, 'I LOVED Jesus.' I had even heard that Jesus loved me and had sung that song too as a kid. Yet I had NO REVELATION of how Jesus could directly impact my life. My faith was in my horoscope.

Psalms 115:4-8 states:

Their idols are silver and gold, the work of mens hands, they have mouths , but they speak not, they have eyes, but they see not; They have ears, but they hear not, noses they have, but they smell not; they have hands, but they handle not; feet have they, but they walk not; neither speak they through their throat. They that make them are like unto them; so is everyone that trusteth in them.

1 Samuel 12:21 states:

Do not turn away after useless idols. They can do you no good, nor can they rescue you, because they are useless.

We were about halfway through the road when I looked to my right and saw a huge mural on the side of a building. It was a picture of a man looking upward with an expression of despair on his face and blood trickling down his face. My heart started racing because I remembered that picture from a nightmare I had.

The vision came crashing in:

When I was 25 years old, I began to attend church and began to know God. Only then did I learn that this lifestyle was not of God. Yet even with that knowledge, the horoscopes were hard to quit and the psychics even harder. The last time I went to a psychic, I had already been in church for a few months and was reading my Bible on a regular basis. In fact, I had just read about King Saul visiting a medium. Though I had knowledge that it was deemed a sin, I lacked understanding and revelation of why within my heart.

I hesitated. "I already paid for it." my sister insisted.

Reluctantly, I agreed.

"One more time," I justified as I walked in.

The reading was uneventful, but that night God would ensure that I received all the understanding and revelation I required for my soul by way of a dream.

In my dream, I walked into an old home. By a windowsill on my left, was a photo of the psychic we had visited that day. She was lying in a bed and staring at the ceiling, with two entities standing and looking down over her. It was as if she was in a trance controlled by the two entities.

Ahead of me, there was a descending stairway, and the lower they went, the darker it became. I started to go down the steps onwards into the darkness of the lower levels. As I got to the bottom of the stairs, I looked to my right, and there was a mural of a man looking upward with blood trickling down his head. There were hundreds of candles lit at the bottom of this mural, and in blood was written, "I pledge my life to you."

Suddenly, a force started lifting me up and down and banging my head on the ceiling. I was frightened, and the force was becoming more violent. I tried calling on the name of Jesus, but the words got stuck in the back of my throat. I kept pushing and pushing, and the words finally broke free, "Jesus! Jesus!"

Immediately, I heard bells approaching ... *ding* ... *ding* ... and I was released and I was safe.

I woke up screaming and crying from this dream. I turned on all the lights in my home and immediately repented for visiting the psychic with my sister that day.

Later that week I read:

<u>Exodus 28 v 34, 35</u>

<u>*34 The gold bells and the pomegranates are to alternate around the hem of the robe. 35 Aaron must wear it when he ministers. The sound of the bells*</u>

will be heard when he enters the Holy Place before the LORD and when he comes out, so that he will not die.

It turned out that the high priests were required to wear bells attached to their holy garments while they were in the temple. Some believe the sound actually kept the priest safe; others believe the bells served as proof to the people that the priest was still alive. Regardless of which meaning one opts for, the sound of the bells in my dream felt safe and that I was alive.

That dream informed me that those two entities had taken over the psychic I had visited that day and allowed her to speak into the lives of those who paid for her services. That dream showed me that those who practice or partake of divination, tarot, or any other form of witchcraft or sooth-saying had knowingly or perhaps unknowingly made a pact with the enemy.

That was the very last time I ever visited a psychic. I thank God every day of my life for His mercy and my freedom.

Have you ever partaken of a psychic reading or something that appeared harmless such as reading your horoscope?

I encourage you today to ask God for forgiveness of those sins, In Jesus name.

Then, the next vision came.

I stood there washing dishes, and all of a sudden, I was filled with fear. Recently in church they had been teaching about the power of praying in tongues, and I had recently been filled with the Holy Spirit with evidence of speaking in tongues.

I started praying in the Spirit to help me overcome the fear I felt inside. Suddenly, I heard a cat screeching, and it ran around my house, in a circle pattern three times before it left. I knew something was wrong, and I was creeped out.

As I continued praying in the Spirit, I put down my sponge, wiped my hands on my pants and walked upstairs to check on my mother. I had recently allowed her back into my house with the condition that she would not bring any tarot cards with her. Though she had agreed, I soon came to understand that the hold of those cards on her would not come into agreement with us so easily.

Though I loved her, this was the day I realized my mother and I would have to part ways. It was not that I didn't want her with me, it was about everything else I was potentially granting access to my home that came along with her activities. Though I had only been in church for about a year, I had gained an important revelation about protecting my children and providing a godly environment by any means necessary—even if it meant parting ways with the woman who birthed me.

In retrospect, at that time I made the best decision I could have made for the level of revelation I had in Christ. But who I am now is different as well as my faith level. My lean on Grace and Mercy is more secure these days.

As we finished crossing the road, I looked back, and the eerie old guy was long gone. The weather had started to clear up, and we could see more light.

As we approached the next street, I started looking around this land. It was too much. I intentionally remained grateful. I tried to always look at the positive and intentionally focus on the beauty of my moment, but this? There were no words for this. The sun was out, and my eyes rested on a big colorful tree to my right.

"Hey Fanci, let's sit over there for a few minutes." I said.

"Now that's a great idea," she replied.

As we sat, we saw pine cones in a multitude of colors. All this beauty surrounded me, yet my mind was filled with not so beautiful things. Worries and doubts kept invading my mind.

My eyes began to water and as I picked up one of the pinecones with my hands and tried putting my focus on its edges, and its shape. Would we ever see Doc again? Could we really do this without him? He had been our guide. Would we see Stacia again? Was Mr. El even real? This entire journey seemed futile, and I needed to get home to my kids.

Quickly I stood up and began to take control of my thoughts and speak the opposite of the doubts my mind was being attacked with. I began to focus on all the amazing things that had already happened on this journey, Stacia, the angels, Doc. I had met Fanci and Mary Sonshine.

"We are gonna make it. Failure is not an option. I can do this; We can do this Fanci!" I looked over at Fanci who was squinting and staring at something ahead in the distance.

Suddenly she said "Hey, do you see that? Look over there."

As we got up, we noticed a figure a few trees down.

We walked over and the closer we drew we saw that it was a woman sitting under a tree. Her face was beaten badly, and her clothes were ripped. We rushed over to her.

"Are you OK?" I asked.

The woman looked up at us. In one hand she gripped a tissue and in the other a picture frame.

"Yes, I am now. Just keep him away from me," she said.

"Who? Keep who away? What's your name?" I asked.

"Tracey," she said.

"What's up? Who do you want to be kept away from?" I asked her, searching through the area visually.

"I was trying to get away from my husband. I had just been admitted into my room, and they were taking me down for x-rays when suddenly my cart bumped against the wall a little too hard and as I was falling, I ended up here," she held her arms up. " I don't even know where I am, but I kept hearing El Shaddai, over and over again. It was almost like an echo. Do you know what that is?" she asked.

Fanci and I looked at each other then back at her. "We don't know El Shaddai, but we had similar things happen to us. We are on our way to see Mr. El and get help. Maybe you could come with us," I said.

"To see who? Where?" asked Tracey, cringing as she lightly touched the corner of her lip, quickly sucking in some air through her teeth.

As Fanci handed her some tissue from her bag, I answered, "We are going to see Mr. El. We were told He could help us. I need help with my identity. Fanci is seeking healing. I am sure He could help you also—to find strength, peace of mind and an escape from your situation." "But who is Mr. El?" asked Tracey.

"We will tell you on the way," said Fanci as we helped Tracey stand on her feet.

"Well, it has to be better than where I've been."

We began to walk.

"Yes, ladies. We are off to see Mr. El, the Wonderful Father of all," I said.

We began to walk, and then we saw the next cross-street. The street name was "Once Upon a Time."

"Well, I know this isn't me," said Fanci.

I shook my head from side to side, 'not me.'

We both turned to look at Tracey who trembled.

"It's OK, Tracey. We are with you," I said.

Fanci and I both took a hold of each of her arms and moved forward. Then the vision came.

Once Upon a Time

Tracey's eyes kept going in and out of focus. She stood up and paced silently around the room as a last attempt to stay awake. She looked over at her children sleeping in their beds and hoped she wouldn't wake them. As she pressed her back against the cool wall and slid down to the floor, she looked at her watch. It was only 3 am; she had a while to go before Frankie would be leaving for work.

"A little bit longer. Come on Tracey, you can do this," she whispered to herself as she pinched herself in yet another attempt to stay awake.

Despite these futile attempts to keep her eyes open, the darkness of the room continued to gently coax her eyes to close for longer periods of time. The rhythmic pattern of her children's breathing lulled her senses, convincing her eyes to surrender to their last flutter.

"WAKE UP! WAKE UP!" Frankie began shouting in her face. He grabbed Tracey's hair and dragged her out of the room. "DIDN'T I TELL YOU? DIDN'T I TELL YOU NOT TO GO TO SLEEP!"

Tracey grabbed at his hands, trying to release some of the strain from his grip on her hair. She struggled to scramble to her feet as he began dragging her toward the kitchen.

"I'm sorry Frankie! Frank, I didn't! I was awake! Please Frank. Please don't!" she cried, trying to muffle her voice and avoid waking up her children.

"I simply asked you not to go to sleep. Why do you make me do this to you, Tracey? Why can't you just do what you're told?!"
Frank grunted as he pushed her down onto a chair at the dining room table.

He slapped her, then quickly grabbed her face, and began to squeeze tightly. As he began to shout, she could feel speckles of his spit hit her face.

"Now sit there and don't move, but you want to go to school! Yeah, OK! Like I'm going to allow you to go back to school and you can't even follow simple instructions! You know you would fail anyways. You're too stupid for all that Tracey. You will never be able to do anything on your own." He grabbed her arm and yanked at it.

"I don't have to be up for another two hours, and now you ruined my sleep. Who do you think you are, interrupting my sleep like that? There's no point in going back to bed now. Just sit there and don't say a thing!" he yelled and shoved her down.

He yanked her up and shoved her toward the kitchen table before turning to his bedroom.

She bit her lower lip as hard as she could to muffle the sounds as she began to shake, and the tears began to fall. How had she gotten to this place? Everything had been so different in the beginning. Once upon a time, she was different.

Suddenly, she heard footsteps coming out of the room.

"Are you crying? Tell me you're not crying!
You're such a baby! 'I want to go to school!' School Tracey?! YOU! Not another word of it. Got it." he said.

With that, he grabbed his jacket and keys and headed out the front door. As was custom, Tracey followed him to the front door and watched him pull out of the driveway.

As she stood on the front porch, her eyes began to water, and she began to feel her head pulsate with pain. Certainly, things had changed. Memories of Frankie gently kneeling before her to tie her shoes were now replaced with memories of her kneeling, trying to stand after a beating.

Every day she was learning a darker shade of misery. Having her family together was all she had ever wanted in life.

"Jesus, show me how," she said as the tears poured down her face.

"Tracey, keep walking. It's OK. We are here. We are with you," Fanci said as she hugged her.

"Is that a picture of your family?" Fanci asked.

"Yes, that is a picture of the family I was fighting so hard for, Fanci," she cried out.

"We can't change the past, but these are the reasons why we keep pressing through. Not just for us, but for our families," Fanci responded, looking at both of us.

Tracey closed her eyes and nodded in agreement. She slowly opened her eyes and said "I'm ready. Let's go," as she put her picture away.

I nodded in agreement; we linked arms, and we continued our journey again.

Chapter 7

Small Beginnings

I was getting anxious, and I wanted to go home. Then we saw our next crossroad, and it read, "The Rooftop Kids."

I took a deep breath. I had 10 siblings who had been through a lot with me. Being dysfunctional would have been a step up for my family. Some had mostly healed, and others had not. All of us had scars. I began to pray in the Spirit as we hit the next vision.

The Rooftop Kids

I could see my siblings sitting in my sister's cozy apartment, watching TV. It was like taking a mini vacation. One weekend, my sister had all types of fashion magazines by the front door. After a few questions, I learned she was going to throw them out. I looked at her and asked her to keep them. When I shared my plan with her, she laughed and said, "You're so stupid, G.G. who are you going to sell those to?"

I laughed too, but I did bring them home with me.   Initially, they just sat there because it turned out I was too embarrassed to go out and sell them. Then one day after school, those magazines served their purpose. I was about 9 years old, and I had come home to find no food, again. My little brother was crying, *again*. My older sister Teri was frustrated with my mother, *again*.

It was a cycle, but this time, I had a plan.

"I'm going to go get us some food," I said, as I went to gather my magazines.

"Shut up, fool," my sister said, laughing, but you could still hear the growing curiosity in her voice.

"What are you going to do?" she inquired.

"I got these magazines from Daisy. She was trying to throw them out, but I'm going to sell them," I said.

My sister's frustration subsided, and she began to laugh louder.

"G.G., shut up! Nobody's gonna buy those stupid magazines. They're old," she laughed.

"Oh yes they will," I said, and laughed out loud too.

"I'm gonna sell them for twenty-five cents each or six for a dollar, and yes, I'm gonna accept food stamps too" I said as I laughed out loud.

She kept laughing at me as though I was joking. Although I laughed as well, it was more out of nervousness. I hoped to God none of my friends were home, because it was my intention to go to all 300-plus apartments of the projects I lived in to sell these magazines and bring back some food.

I quickly gathered the magazines in a milk crate and placed the milk crate on an old skateboard. I began pushing the crate out the front door right over to my neighbor's house. I felt embarrassed initially, but that ended shortly after I made my first sale.

I stood in front of my neighbor's door with my crate, al, and named my price. She stared at my magazines, and asked in a nervous voice, "I don't have money, but will you take food stamps?"

I could see the shame in her eyes, and instantly I felt better because I was not alone.

"Of course, I take food stamps," I said with a huge smile, thinking. *'No taxes. More money for me.'*

I walked that day from apartment to apartment until all my magazines were sold. I had a product, and they had a desire. Afterwards, I counted the combination I had of food stamps, cash and change as I headed over to the corner market and grabbed some sandwich meat, bread and pop. I was so grateful as I walked home with the spoils of my victory that day. My family would eat.

I learned the principle.

of supply and demand. Shortly after, I repeated the skill, replacing the magazines with different products and skills. For some I became a babysitter, for others the local fortune teller. I hosted several raffles, some of which I intentionally won. "Heathen!" One may think. Why yes, yes, I was, and at that time, unapologetically so.

It was through those moments that I learned there were three ways I could have handled the issue of lack in my life:

1. I could want but settle for less.

2. I could hurt others to get what I wanted.

3. I could always press past the appearance of nothing and find the hidden something.

And that's what I did. I developed that mindset throughout my lifetime and got really good at finding that "something."

I smiled as I started feeling appreciative of my upbringing.

As we continued, I began to think of my siblings again. As each sibling grew older and was able to fend adequately for themselves, they left home and began the journey of conquering their own demons while trying to find their place in this world.

I sighed as I remembered the times my brothers and sisters left our house one by one. Each time one left, I cried for days because even though we grew up not having much, they were more than enough for me. They were my heroes. Though they couldn't always see it for themselves,
each one of them had a gifting that helped shape me.

Celebrate

Up ahead, I heard loud music and kids playing. A group of kids began running around us; excitedly setting up some kind of stage. Then I remembered:

We had dressed up, and we had set up a stage for a neighborhood concert. It was the boys versus the girls. My brothers had gotten hold of some spray paint from our neighbors and carved wood into the shape of guitars and other musical instruments. There was a wooden drum set, borrowed Christmas lights, and my mom's stereo. Before long, the side of our house was filled with all the project kids to come watch us jam out and battle.

That night, we excitedly performed and sang to our favorite jams from Madonna, Janet Jackson to Metallica, and Stryper as the neighborhood kids watched. Despite the odds we faced as children, we could still find beauty and creativity in the world.

We had little but there were moments when we came together and were stronger, and we overcame.

Then the next vision came, and my sister Daisy jogged right past me:

Daisy

She could barely breathe, but she had to keep moving. Today was important. It was the kids' first day of school. Jogging with two paper bags full of school supplies proved to be quite the challenge, but she had to get going. She couldn't wait on her ride anymore. Momentarily, she put down the bags and pulled her hoodie tighter around her head. The drizzle was threatening to turn into rain and had quickly won the battle against her hair, as she noticed her curls beginning to frizz in front of her eyes.

"Oh well," she thought.

It was a good thing she had triple-bagged the supplies. She had to hurry up because the kids would be getting on their buses soon. She began coughing, and an audible wheeze made its presence known. She hadn't been able to do as much as she would have liked to this year, but it was still more than the previous years. She had managed to buy them all shoes and two outfits each to start off the year with—didn't seem like a lot, but there were seven of them. Every penny added up.

She was grateful she had a husband who understood her family's situation. He loved them just as much as she did. As the rain began to pour down and soak her clothes, she kept focused on how excited they had been when she took them shopping for school clothes. Her baby sister Penelope had been waiting outside by the parking lot of their complex and her eyes had lit up when she saw her.

"A little more to go; just a little more," she encouraged herself.

Suddenly, one of the paper bags ripped. The same sudden movement that helped her catch the contents of the ripped bag instantly betrayed her and caused her foot to slip on the wet pavement. She felt her bottom dampen as she sat in the puddle that had no problem accepting her company. She felt a sting in her eyes as a tear escaped.

"Not now, Daisy, sh*t," she said to herself as she wiped her wet face with her damp sleeve.

"Dang it," she said and then wiped her hot tears away from her face. She quickly got back up and kept running.

Though it was only a couple miles away, the rain was slowing her down and playing tricks on her mind. She kept jogging. Almost there. Soon she saw the entrance to their apartments. Suddenly, the fact that she was wet, and wheezing didn't matter as she felt relief.

As she opened the front door, Penelope yelled, "Daisy!" and ran up to her to give her a hug.

Daisy was Penelope's favorite person. Penelope looked down at her nylons and new shoes. She was gonna start the school year with a set of new clothes. It was getting late, but she knew Daisy would show up because she always looked after them.

The excitement in the room was comparable to a Christmas morning, and that was Daisy's favorite holiday. All the kids huddled around Daisy as she began to divvy up the school supplies. As each kid grabbed their share, they hugged her and ran out the front door to catch the bus.

"Thank you, Daisy!"

"Daisy, Thanks!"

Daisy was always there. These moments together with her siblings were well worth every cent and every struggle. Suddenly, the odor of stale cigarettes filled the room. Her mother emerged wearing a blue nightgown. She yawned, and rubbed her eyes as she smudged mascara farther down her face. The smell of alcohol coming off her mother's pores invaded the room, and she said to Daisy, "You know you have asthma. You should not have come."

Just then, Penelope ran up to her big sister and wrapped her arms around her, smiling "Thank you, Daisy, I love you!" Then she, too, ran out grinning and wide smiled, ready to have the best year ever.

Daisy turned to speak to her mother, but she had already retreated into her room. Letting out a big sigh, Daisy headed outside as well. She had to hurry back home herself. She still had to be at work in a couple of hours.

She was only 19, yet she felt the weight of the world on her shoulders.

She had to keep going, and she would keep going. Nothing would stop her from helping her siblings. She was the only chance the bunch had left. They had all been through so much already.

As she passed the entry gate out of the impoverished community, she focused on the road ahead. The only evidence of the rainstorm that remained were the puddles she was avoiding. At that moment, she looked up at the sky, and a brilliant thought crossed her mind. Just as the sun was waging war on the rain clouds to shine, she too would wage war for a better future. Failure was not an option. She knew one day it would be different and with that knowledge, she continued her race.

2 Timothy 4:7

I have fought the good fight, I have finished the race, I have kept the faith

Chapter 8

Closing In

I wondered how Doc was doing. Was he ok?

Then, up ahead on the side of the road we saw a line of long mirrors floating in the air. Standing in front of one of them we saw a tall muscular man staring into one of them in a trancelike state.

Fanci and I stopped and stared at each other. "What is this all about?" whispered Fanci as she quickly turned away from the mirrors and moved past them quickly, avoiding her reflection.

"Fanci why are you...?" I also whispered, observing her reaction, but was cutoff.

"... me without hair. I don't want to see what that looks like. I haven't seen a mirror in a while. I just want to get to Mr. El to get healed," she said.

Tracey walked closer to the man and suddenly caught a glimpse of herself in the mirrors, "I know I definitely need to get my hair done," as she fidgeted with her hair.

I placed my palm on my forehead, and quickly redirected my attention to the gentleman. He had distinguished tattoos stretching from the upper part of his neck all the way down both arms. He had wavy dark hair and prominent almond eyes.
He was quite attractive.

"Hello, sir? Hi! My name is G.G."

He looked over at me and just when I thought he was about to smile, he slipped back into his trance facing the mirror.

I took a few steps closer to him and stared harder into the mirror. Fanci wasn't the only one who was insecure about her looks, but unlike Tracey, it wasn't what I looked like that caught my attention.

Initially, I could just see his reflection but as I continued to focus I slowly began to see castles in the sky.

"Sir, excuse me. Sir. Are you okay?" Fanci raised her voice.

The castles appeared to be growing in size and definition. I physically turned around, but there was nothing behind us. So I turned back to the reflection in the mirror, and suddenly I could see more. The door to the castle opened up and suddenly, I could see clearly.

I sat behind a desk, writing, and as the image zoomed in, I could see that I seemed to be writing a story. But what was I writing? I started to squint and suddenly the lettering became clear.

The writing read:

shuffle, shuffle the cards go anxiously
waiting for her future to be told

shuffle, shuffle what did
she see lies from
demons
fallacies she believed

shuffle, shuffle she can't put
them down
more faith in those cards than the One with the
crown

shuffle, shuffle
What did she gain? mangled
emotions,
a paranoid brain

yet she kept shuffling, spirit
diminishing within,
stolen moments of beauty heart full
of sin

shuffle, shuffle she can't
put them down saturated
her soul

with alcohol and fun around town,

a generational blessing, polluted with

a generational curse

*five scores of shuffling
but I ended it all*

*NO SHUFFLING for me nor ANY of mine
passing on my faith in my King and my
love for Christ and slowly but surely His
Spirit grows within
helping me take back my family and friends I
won't stop praying 'till all the shuffling
ends
and ALL of my people are free from a life of
shuffling in sin!*

I looked away from the mirror and gripped onto the gentlemen standing next to me. I was trying to speak, but my words would not come out.

I had been contemplating writing a book, but the vision in this mirror showed so much more than that.

"Fanci," I said, and I slightly stumbled over to her as I kept looking.

"Fanci, Tracey look at this, you gotta see this" I said as I called them over.

"What is it? G.G., I'm not looking. No." I kept pulling on her arm and abruptly she answered.

"Fine!" said Fanci reluctantly, as she turned to face the mirror.

Maybe one day, she thought, *I'll be able to look in the mirror again and feel some kind of beauty.* Then Fanci's mouth dropped open wide as the first scene hit her eyes:

Fashion Show

The music was pumping, and the energy was high. Click-flash, click-flash! Photographers snapped pictures and reporters scribbled fervently as they tried to capture the entire scene with all its colors and beauty. The slim girls headed out on the catwalk one by one, each strutting their own unique interpretation of beauty. They were dressed in the latest trends and colors by one of the hottest designers that season.

Behind the scenes, the energy was even higher as the models would quickly change wardrobe and makeup during the show. "Ms. Fanci, excuse me. May I speak with you for a moment? Can I ask you a couple of questions when you have a moment please?" someone asked.

Fanci looked up as she realized it was the senior editor from *Couture La Rue.* They were a major fashion resource in the beauty industry. Instantly,

Fanci realized this could bring her to a whole new level in her career. Fanci attempted to focus on applying just the right amount of blush needed to create the depth and dimension that would accentuate the model's high cheekbones. "Sure, I can do that," Fanci said as she smiled and applied a tinted lip balm. A color that finished the look.

"What would you like to know?" she asked.

The reporter looked at her and laughed, stating, "Ms. Fanci, if you don't mind, I'd like to discuss a career opportunity with you, set up some time for a few photos and an interview over lunch ."

Fanci's heart skipped a beat. "Absolutely. No problem," she replied with a smile.

The slender lady handed her a card. "Great! Here's my card. Please call me in the morning so we can schedule that," she said.

Just then, the model with the cheekbones got up and started heading to the runway. Fanci reached over and took the card and shook the well-manicured hand while thanking her.

"No, thank *you*, Ms. Fanci. We've had our eye on you for a while now. The pleasure is all mine," she said.

As she walked away, Fanci was jolted back into the task at hand when suddenly, the next model excitedly popped into her makeup chair.

"Ms. Fanci, I'm so excited to be working with you," said the model.

Fanci, however, still staring back, was not focusing on the model's words. Instead, she had begun to intensely focus on the model's bone structure and could see the colors boldly popping off her face like a piece of art waiting to be painted.

Her gift was clear, and with time it was becoming more refined. She had the ability to create beauty with anything her hands touched. She continued working and kept creating beauty for the rest of the night. Beauty had become her work, her art, and a huge part of her life. Yet the kind of beauty she possessed could not be applied, could not be fabricated, and it could not be bought at a store. This gift for beauty she possessed had come at a huge price and had been acquired only after winning one of the ugliest and most beastly battles of her life.

"What is this?" asked Fanci as she stood at the mirror.

"I'm not sure," I said.

"What is it? What are you guys seeing? What do you guys see?" asked Tracey, looking again, and squinting her eyes. "I don't see anything but us."

We didn't understand why Tracey couldn't see anything, but after changing positions from sitting to standing and moving from near to far we decided we would focus on the man in the mirror again.

"Sir. Hello? Can you hear me?" I asked as I tapped both shoulders and waved my hands in front of him.

"We can't stay here all night," said Tracey, "we gotta keep it moving."

"G.G. She's right. We can't stay. We are losing time." Fanci agreed.

"My friend, I don't know how you got here, but I need you to snap out of it. Will you please look at me?" I said as I gently touched his face with both sides of my hands.

'Sir, I don't know what you have been through, but if you can understand me, I need you to look at me."

Slowly, he began to turn his gaze to me and began to smile. He lifted both arms and placed them on my shoulders. Just as he was about to speak, the expression in his eyes began to change and they filled with a mixture of anger and pain. He fell onto the floor and began to cry, inconsolably.

"Help me. Help me please."

We all gathered around him, placing our hands on him as gently as possible.

"Hey, sir, please stop and look at me. I am here. I am with you. STOP." I said gently but as firmly as possible, placing his hands in my hands and locking eyes with him.

Suddenly he stopped. As he began to calm down, I began to introduce myself.

"My name is G.G., this is Fanci," I said.

"And I am Tracey." Tracey piped in, "We are on our way to see Mr. El, The Wonderful Father of All."

He slowly began to wipe his tears and slowed his breathing.

"Who? What?" he cried, "Who are you gonna go see?"

"Mr. El. We are on our way to see Mr. EL and no matter what, if you come with us, we won't leave you."

He stared at me, closely, and started sitting up. "Are you for real? I've been here for so long. Alone. My name is Grover."

"I am so embarrassed. My apologies, ladies. I've just been alone for so long. Even as people walked by and sometimes stopped and sat around me. They would simply point fingers and whisper or laugh at me." He slowly rose to his feet and continued composing himself.

"I was on my way to see him once, Mr. El. It seems like so long ago, but I kept getting distracted. Different people, different things kept coming up, and..." He looked down. "I was around a lot of people. I've done things that now I wish I could change."

He stared down at the ground and ran his hand over his right upper arm revealing elongated scars cloaked within his tattoos.

"The people I was around weren't doing much better than me. One day I woke up, and I decided I was tired of doing the same thing over and over again. I wanted my life to change, but I didn't know how or what to do. So, I asked God to help me change everything and to give me a chance to make my life better.

I was determined as I started out on my journey to reach Mr. El. Then, I ran into these mirrors. I didn't think much at first, but as I stared into the mirror I saw a castle in the sky, but only in the mirror's reflection. As my focus became more intent, the castle grew and as it drew closer the castle doors opened and I started seeing all kinds of amazing things. I saw myself surrounded by the people I loved. I was attending the local university. I was a sportscaster. I was getting ready to walk away and continue my journey to Mr. El, I couldn't."

Grover continued to tell us about the people he had met on this journey, and we told him of ours. We told him all about ours, including how we had lost Doc and our hope that not only could Mr. El help us personally but also to help us recover Doc. After we spent a little more time exchanging our stories with one another, and after a little more encouragement, Grover agreed to join us on our quest.

As we continued to walk and talk, we came across a road called "Expiration Date."

"Well, it's not me. The devil is a lie, because I know not one of us is expiring, in Jesus name." said Fanci with a chuckle.

We stared at each other and let out a nervous laugh. Then we locked arms with one another, took a deep breath and simultaneously stepped onto the cross street. We chose to continue our journey with courage and Faith.

Expiration Date

It turned out my mother was into parenting as equally as I was into obedience. I was living a hard-knock life. After the last time I ran away, it was decided I would be sent to live with family in Michigan. The day I was to board the plane, waiting in the airport lobby, my crew of friends showed up encouraging me to run away *again,* but at that moment, I knew if I stayed, I was headed towards a dark future and chaos. I also knew if I chose to board the plane, though my future was unknown, it could at least be a chance for something better. I was 14 years old when I chose to leave my mother's side.

Although I missed my old friends: every day I was being exposed to new experiences, making new friends, and I was grateful.

On one such occasion, I received a call from one of my new friends, Gecolle, who invited me to dinner with her mom. I quickly accepted in excitement. Not only was I grateful for the friendship but I could count the number of times, on the one hand, I had been to a restaurant. To me, going to a restaurant without a special occasion was a special occasion. I made sure to mind my manners and even though I was told that I could order whatever I wanted on the menu, in my view, I didn't want to be more of a burden, so I ordered the most inexpensive item. There was no way I would impose any more than I already was.

Shortly after, the waiter brought my order of burger and fries, and I enthusiastically poured ketchup all over. Everything looked so good and as I took a bite of one of my fries, my chewing instantly slowed down. I didn't understand what was wrong, because honestly, even ketchup was a commodity growing up—but I recognized that this just didn't taste like ketchup. Quickly I gulped down some of my Coke to get the taste out of my mouth. I sat there, but I couldn't bring myself to say anything. I tried again, grabbing another fry, but the rancid taste was still there. I sat there and focused on my burger and scoured my plate for any remnant fries that I had missed with the ketchup.

Noticing, Mrs. Hall asked, "Is there something wrong with your fries?"

Hesitantly, I nodded my head and said, "I think there's something wrong with the ketchup." Mrs. Hall took a bite of a fry and immediately grabbed a napkin and spit it out.

"Do you want different fries? I can call the waiter."

As she began to motion for the waiter, I immediately shook my head.

"No, it's OK ... it's not that bad," I said, smiling. There was no way I was going to complain.

I grabbed another fry and ate it quickly, simultaneously suppressing any negative facial expressions.

How could I complain? I was so grateful for this blessing. Though the fries were disgusting, I refused to be of any more inconvenience to these kind people who had generously gone out of their way to include me in their dinner plans.

"G.G., you don't have to eat those," Mrs. Hall stated.

"It's OK, ma'am. It's not too bad," I answered as I ate another fry.

As I continued to walk farther with my new pals, I remembered one night as I was soaking my pillow with tears, The Holy Spirit gave me the revelation that much like the expired ketchup that day, I had also began to accept various people and their behaviors into my life that were spoiled, expired or no longer good for me.

Though I was postured in gratitude, my complacency with the level of "better" I had achieved combined with the fear of failure and of the unknown were holding me captive. Was it right to expect anymore? I had acquired so much already and come a long way away from my project days. Who was I to expect even more? Was this desire for something more wrong for me to have, after all God had done for me already?

My thoughts were all over the place. I had no idea why this was happening to me, why God allowed me to be placed in this Land of Purpose, or really who all these new people were around me. Beginning to feel anxious, I quickly redirected my focus back on the journey ahead of us.

Once we had crossed the street, we all sat down to rest and collect ourselves for a moment.

Meanwhile, Jez was watching all along.

"We can't let them make it to see Mr. El. If they make it, I will never be able to stop them then," she said.

There were dark forces with her.

"We need to get them off the white road. If they stay on the white narrow road, they will be sure to reach their destination. I have thrown my best at them. I have attacked them with some of their most painful wounds, and they just won't quit. They keep pressing through it all. But what I have next will surely take them out."
Thinking, she suddenly said,

"I KNOW! They haven't been taking time to pray and have had nothing to eat. They won't make it out of here this time. I need two teams. Team one, go and attack now. We need to slow them down to buy us some time. Team two, draw near," she said.

They began to huddle and strategize.

Chapter 9

Deception

After we had rested, we continued on our journey once again. Grover continued to speak of his childhood and things he had struggled with. He spoke of different disappointments he had endured and different mistakes he had made. We all encouraged one another and allowed each other to voice truths without fear of judgment.

We had been walking and talking for quite a while but had gradually begun to slow down.

"Guys, I'm hungry. I'm gonna have to get something to eat," said Tracey.

"I know. We have been walking for almost six hours," said Fanci.

"Will we ever get there?" said Tracey.

"Look over there. There is a sign lit up that says, 'Sizzling Eats.' Let's grab something and go," said Fanci.

"Hmm … guys, I don't know. That place is off the white road, and Stacia told me to make sure I stayed on the narrow white road," I said.

"But look, the road is a little… white-ish. It's just for a minute. I'm hungry," said Tracey.

I remained quiet as I heard my own stomach grumble.

The entire time, Jez and her demons were watching from behind the restaurant.

"Something feels weird, guys," I said.

"Come on, G.G. If we hurry up, we'll be alright," said Tracey.

I gave in, and we walked up to the restaurant. The people behind the counter seemed harmless enough. They didn't smile, but they didn't snarl either, so I figured, *meh, we're cool.*

We began to order food, and as we sat down I started to relax, until I took my first bite. Immediately, I started getting a headache.

"What's wrong G.G.?" asked Fanci.

"I don't know. I don't feel too well," I said.

Grover reached over to me and looked down at my food,

"Well look at it. There is no way I would eat that." He was pointing at green speckles in the food.

"What is that? G.G. Don't eat that. Stop eating that." He picked up both of our plates and threw them in the trash can near us.

My head was pounding, and I carefully laid it down on the table. Grover headed to the front counter.

"I'm just fine," said Tracey as she began to eat, and eat and eat. Suddenly Tracey appeared to not be able to eat enough. She started reaching over for Fanci's food.

"Uhhhh, Tracey. Are you okay?" asked Fanci as she started pulling her plate away.

"I'm fine," through bites of more food Tracey replied. She ate and drank her food. As she was masticating her food her face started to turn beet red, and suddenly she spit it up out of her mouth.

"Guys, what have we done?" I muttered, realizing that Tracey was not herself. I attempted to lift my head off the table, but my head throbbed more.

Fanci had not taken a bite from her food at all, and said, "This isn't right. We need to leave."

She attempted to get up, and she was pushed back down forcefully.

I did not understand what was happening. I couldn't stand up. I closed my eyes and opened them again, but still could not see anything aside from my three friends.

"Grover!" I yelled out for him, but Grover suddenly crouched on the ground covering his head.

We were in trouble.

I closed my eyes again and could hear Doc saying, "Pray in the Spirit. When something doesn't feel right, you pray in the Spirit till that feeling goes away."

I began to pray and though I did not feel better initially, I kept praying. I opened my eyes one more time, and this time I could see that demons surrounded us.

One was touching my head. Another one was holding Fanci down while another one kept forcing Tracey to pick up another scoop of food and shoveling it down her throat.

"You are so hungry, aren't you? You just can't get enough, can you? It tastes so good." The minion kept laughing and picking her hand up and shoveling more food down her throat.

Fanci kept trying to get up.

"Pray in the Spirit!" I yelled, "We are under attack. 'Father God, I ask that you give them eyes to see. Allow them to see through your eyes, Lord, so they may understand the importance of prayer in this very moment,'"

Grover looked over at me and suddenly he could see too. He began to pray and managed to get on his feet. Covered by demons he kept pushing his way towards me. There was one demon specifically that was reaching down to his heart. As the demon squeezed harder, Grover stopped for a moment, grimaced, and stopped for a moment. He then clenched his fist and kept pressing towards us.

Fanci began praying, too.

Then suddenly, Tracey could see too. She started coughing and began to recite "Our Father."

The more my head hurt, the more intense I would pray. As we continued to pray and praise, a sweet aroma began to arise. Then suddenly, Stacia appeared.

She said, "You are on the wrong road. This is a road of deception. I can help you, but I can't do it all. You MUST begin to move despite the pain you may feel. NOW IS NOT THE TIME FOR TEARS. GET UP AND WALK OUT OF HERE."

She stared at the demons attacking Grover and began commanding them to leave in the name of Jesus. As she disappeared, so did the demons torment Grover. Continuously praying and walking towards me, he took hold of my arm and pulled me up to my feet. Then we walked over to Fanci, then Tracey. Arm in arm, fervently praying, we walked out of there.

Once outside, with our eyes wide open, we quickly but carefully moved forward and made our way back to the narrow white road.

Suddenly, the afflictions came to an end...mostly. We opened our eyes and found that we were standing smack dab in the middle of a narrow white road.

Cast to the side of the road, was a moldy loaf of bread. There was no restaurant. There were no waiters.

"Now that's nasty," Fanci said as she pointed to the moldy bread. Tracey kicked the loaf of bread, and it turned into a greenish powder.

"This was a huge mistake, and it could have cost us everything," said Fanci.

"Hey, do you hear that?" asked Grover and in the distance, we could hear music.

"We must be getting closer to Golden City. Let's go," I said.

As we began to run towards the sound. Grover crouched over struggling to breathe, grasping at his chest.

"What's wrong? Sit down. What is it?" I asked.

He bent over with both hands on his knees.

"I'm having a hard time breathing," he said.

We moved towards him, but when I touched him, my heart began beating fast. Horrific images and thoughts began to invade my mind. My own head began to hurt, and I quickly backed away.

As I took a few minutes to gather my wits, Tracey and Fanci continued to assist Grover.

"What's going on Grover?" asked Fanci.

I continued to battle to focus on something peaceful or beautiful. Fanci looked over at me and then back at Grover.

"Let's just take a few more moments to pray, guys," Fanci said.

Grover was still trying to catch his breath. Together, we managed to get him on his feet. We all held hands together and prayed. Slowly, the images stopped, and Grover's respirations became regular.

"Guys, I don't think I can run anymore, but I *can* walk."

"By hook or by crook, by walk or a crawl, we will get there, ONCE AND FOR ALL," declared Fanci.

"Crook? Really Fanci?" asked Tracey. We all stared at each other and began to laugh.

Together, we continued on our journey.

Chapter 10

Golden City

Though the music was steadily getting louder, we were having to take multiple breaks to give Grover an opportunity to rest.

We finally arrived at a huge castle that was all white, with gold trimming. We walked to the door and knocked on it. A huge angel suddenly appeared and frightened us all.

"No need to be afraid," said the angel. "My name is Gabriel. How may I help you?" he asked. "We have come to see Mr. El," I said.

"Someone told us that He could help us," said Fanci.

"Do you believe that He can?" asked Gabriel.

"I don't know," said Tracey.

"Well, I apologize, but you can't come in then," said Gabriel.

"What do you mean we can't come in?" I asked.

"Anyone that comes to the Father must believe that He is, and that He is a rewarder of them who diligently seek Him. If you don't believe that He can help you, then you won't receive the help. Faith is always necessary," said Gabriel.

"But wait, we do believe. Our faith is evidenced by our works in coming here in the first place. We came because we believed what Stacia told us," I said.

"Yup," chimed in Fanci, "I know I believe! I just got tired on the way, but I believe all right,"

"Well, I know I believe." Grover chimed in.

"One of you does not," said Gabriel.

Then he looked over at Tracey right before he shut the door. We all stared at Tracey. In the background the crickets suddenly began to chirp, and Fanci placed her hand on her forehead and looked down.

"Uhhh, Tracey. What does he mean that you don't believe, Tracey?" I asked quietly and placed my forefinger on my lips.

"Well, I don't exactly know who Mr. El is, and I'm not exactly sure I believe He can help me," said Tracey.

Fanci spoke up, "Tracey, what do you believe in then?"

Tracey clasped her hands in front of her while she shuffled her feet. "I don't know. I don't think I really believe in anything at all," she said.

"Tracey, do you believe that Jesus Christ is your Lord and Savior?" I asked.

Tracey said, "I never really thought of it."

"Well, you better start thinking about it now," said Fanci snapped, catching an attitude.

"Tracey!" I spoke sternly, "What do you mean?"

Fanci rolled her eyes.

Then Grover chimed in.

"Ok. OK. Everyone calm down. Take a deep breath. Tracey, it's ok." He placed his arm around her. "Tracey, do you believe that Jesus Christ lived and that He died as a living sacrifice for your sins?"

Tracey said, "Oh, that? Yes, of course I do," she said, smiling. "That's why I always talk to Him—because I know He is there."

"OK then. Have you ever asked Him to be your Lord and Savior, Tracey?" I asked.

"Well … no, not officially. I didn't know that I had to," said Tracey.

Fanci sighed out loud and placed her hand on her forehead one more time and looked away.

"OK then, it is very simple. All you have to do is to ask for forgiveness of your sins and ask Him to be your Lord and personal Savior and invite Him into your heart," Grover said.

"OK, I can do that," said Tracey with a smile on her face.

We all closed our eyes and began to pray. Tracey repeated my words and invited the Lord into her heart.

Right as we ended the prayer with "In Jesus' name, amen," Gabriel suddenly appeared again.

"That's much better. Now you all may come in," said Gabriel as he opened the door.

What we saw next was one of the most beautiful sights we had ever beheld. Everything was pearly white.

"Are we in heaven?" asked Tracey.

"This is the Land of Purpose Headquarters also known as The Golden City," said Gabriel winking his eye.

Anxious for Answers

We could hear praise and worship music playing in the background. There were so many angels singing and praising, and as soon as they saw us they quickly rushed over and began ministering to our needs.

After being given an opportunity to rest, Gabriel returned and led us to see Mr. El. My heart was beating fast. Finally, it was the moment we had been waiting for. The room was so bright that it was almost blinding. Suddenly a warmth came over us.

"Oh dear," said Gabriel, "I almost forgot about these." He handed us some dark glasses. "Nobody can really look at Me. El face to face. Not if they want to return home." We all looked at each other and quickly grabbed the glasses.

"What you will see now is the room with virtual imagery, and though it is precisely accurate, you will only see Mr. El in his virtual human form. Please remember, do not remove your glasses. Not if you want to return to your homes."

We all nodded. We continued to take a few steps forward and the closer we got to the center of the room, the stronger the presence got. A gentle presence began to rise, and it felt as though we were walking on clouds. As we looked around in awe, we heard Gabriel say, "Mr. El, you have some guests."

"I do? Well, bring them along," said Mr. El as he arose from a golden throne.

For a moment all we could do was stare in awe at the scenery. I began to introduce myself when Mr. El smiled and nodded his head.

He said, "I know who you are. You've come for my help. You, G.G., need help in establishing your identity. Fanci needs healing. Tracey needs peace and strength to escape an abusive relationship and all of you long to have your family united, and Grover. Grover and I will have our own conversation."

We all glanced at each other then back at Grover then back at Mr. El.

"Though it is G.G. requesting help establishing her identity, it would appear that all of you have identity problems, and I have already done more than enough." Mr. El said.

"What do you mean? We were told that you could help us, and you never mentioned Doc. Doc was taken. We need help getting him back." I exclaimed in shock. Fanci and Tracey stood there with their mouths dropped open.

"One moment. I will explain, G.G. I have already provided you with solutions. Two thousand years ago, I sent my Son. He is everything you need and more. In Him is all the faith, the love, the healing, the safety, the wisdom, the peace, and provision you could ever need, and so much more. All you must do is trust and believe what my Book says. Apply The Word to your life. I have given you authority through my Son's name to defeat Jez and any demon that comes against you or your loved ones. As a matter of fact, they are already defeated.

I have been watching you and Doc was never in danger. Why are you running from Jez? She has already been defeated. She only possesses the power of illusion, suggestion, and deception. Jesus Christ redeemed you from the curse of the law when He hung on the tree. Apply that redeeming love to your life. You have everything you seek; you just have to go and take it back. Take back everything that the enemy stole from you. I have given you authority, and you must not be afraid, because I am with you. I have already redeemed you. It is your job to stand up to Jez and take back what's yours. Once you have returned with Doc we will see about getting y'all back home. Now, if you don't mind, I have an entire universe to look after. Grover, would you accompany me please?" said Mr. El as he winked and started to walk away.

"But wait, Mr. El, can I ask one more question?"

Mr. El nodded.

"Do you know who Jehovah-Rapha is? Or what El Shaddai is?"

I looked over at Grover as he stepped away from us and began to walk towards Mr. El.

"Of course, G.G.," he laughed out loud, "I will gladly explain. They are all me."

We all stared blankly at him.

He smiled and elaborated a little bit more.

"Since the beginning of time, I have helped humanity in many ways, and because of this I have many names."

"Ok!" He threw his arms up. "Some people know me as Elohim. Others as *El `Elyon* (Most High God), *El Shaddai* (God Almighty), there is also *El `Olam*

(Everlasting God), there is *El Hai* (Living God), *El Ro'i* (God of Seeing), *El Elohe Israel* (God, the God of Israel), *El Gibbor* (God of Strength). I have quite a few names. So yes G.G. I go by Mr. El for short. Did that help you?" He smiled at us sincerely.

I smiled back and nodded my head yes.

Grover smiled and said, "I'll be back, guys."

Then he walked away, side by side with Mr. El.

We stood there watching them as they exited, and then suddenly Gabriel appeared.

"Ladies, I will show you the way out." Gabriel said. "Oh no, hey, we have to wait for Grover," we said.

Gabriel smiled and stepped through a big golden door and came back out with a book that radiated a bright light.

"Grover has been sent on another assignment. Trust that the only thing you need is this," responded Gabriel, handing us a Bible.

We had not envisioned Grover not being part of this journey. He had become one of our friends and just then, Grover came walking quickly towards us holding our backpacks.

"Hey guys!" Grover yelled out. "I have great news! Mr. El has some stuff for me to do around here, so I won't be able to join y'all this time, but y'all almost left these behind."

Grover began handing us the bags.

"Grover? What? Are you serious" we asked quickly.

"Guys, You guys will be fine without me. Besides, you'll be back before you know it."

After a little more discussion, we came to agree with Grover's perspective.

As we headed out, we noticed a garden to the left of us and quickly ran over to it. To our delight, we saw a variety of fruits and vegetables and quickly picked a few and threw them in our bags.

Then, we continued our journey.

Chapter 11

Reversing the Curse

"..and then there were three," said Fanci kicking a rock in front of her.

We had been quiet since leaving Grover behind.

"Hey guys! We need to be happy. Rejoice! Grover is well, and we will be back together soon enough. We got to Mr. El. We made it to The Land Of Purpose Headquarters! We have so much to be grateful for!" Tracey interjected.

"You're actually right Tracey. We are more than halfway home," Fanci added.

I quickly wiped my eyes, stopped in my tracks, and started doing ten jumping jacks. Tracey and Fanci both looked at me with quizzical expressions. I took a deep breath in through my nose and blew it out my mouth 3 times.

"Whaaaat?" I shouted, erupting in laughter. "It's just something I do. I've never seen someone feeling depressed while doing jumping jacks. You should try it sometime."

I laughed, and they joined in my laughter while they continued to tease me about my technique. "Guys, we have to find Jez and get Doc back, but how will we find her?" asked Fanci, putting her palm to her face.

None of us had an answer.

Then, suddenly Stacia appeared. She could see the look of discouragement on our faces.

"Oh, thank God, Stacia! Yes! We are so glad to see you! Yes!" We all excitedly shouted out and ran to her.

Stacia smiled.

"You made it! I knew you guys would!" said Stacia, full of excitement.

"Yes, but Stacia, I still have so many more questions. Like, how are we going to find Jez? What were those mirrors we passed earlier on our journey? How come we could see all these amazing things?" I asked.

" G.G. Those mirrors are anointed mirrors. Before God put you here on this earth, He created you with a purpose in mind. Those mirrors hold the ability to show you some of the wonderful things God has prepared for you. It showed you exactly what it could be if you fight the good fight of faith for it, whatever your 'it' is," said Stacia.

"After you have retrieved Doc, and have made it back home, then, the real battle begins. G.G. You will need to go back and take everything you have learned on this journey and apply it to your life. Once you begin to do that, it will all make sense to you. Once you begin to walk in the power of who you are because of who you are in Christ. Not Jez nor any other minion will be able to stand up against you when you walk in your authority. Not in this land nor anywhere else. You are all God's workmanship. It is time for you to break the generational curses that your bloodlines have been plagued with. This is spiritual warfare, and you ladies must begin to use the weapons He has equipped you with. You are going to have to pray in the Spirit, fast and watch your words—confess the right things. There is power in words. Jez is just a representative of Satan. They have no new tricks. You must remember to use your weapons."

Stacia told us to remember these two scriptures:

> *For the weapons of our warfare are not carnal, but mighty through God to the pulling down of strong holds. -II Corinthians 10:4*

"The weapons aren't natural, so you cannot fight naturally," she said.

> *No man can enter into a strong man's house and spoil his goods, except he will f first bind the strong man; and then he will spoil his house. -Mark 3:27*

"You have to bind the strong man first. You must go in the authority of Jesus Christ."

"Ladies, it will be essential for you to learn scripture so you can pull on its power. The words from the Word contain power when spoken in

Faith. Just like a sword, the Word cuts away at anything attempting to come against you. So many times, people train to be physically strong, but they remain spiritually weak. The fact is that everything in the physical world has a spiritual root. Also remember that when the battle feels long, pull from the Word of God, including scriptures such as:

> *But if (the thief) be found, he shall restore sevenfold; he shall give all the substance of his house. -Proverbs 6:31*

"You got that, ladies? Sevenfold," she added as she stared at every single one of us.

We all just looked at each other as we took in her words.

Stacia followed that by saying, "OK, ladies. It is time to reverse the curse. Let the journey begin."

Then before we could say another thing, she was gone.

I couldn't help but think of the spiritual weapons she had mentioned. The power of words was something that had been unknowingly implemented in my life ever since I was a little girl. Many times, people unknowingly say things that curse their own well-being and situations. We fail to acknowledge or gain a true revelation that the life we helped to create with our words. Words are powerful.

Just then the skies began to grow dark, and thunder could be heard from a distance.

"Well guys, now what?" I asked.

"Maybe we should look up some scriptures before it starts to rain," said Fanci.

We all huddled in a circle.

The wind began to pick up, and Tracey took the Bible and opened it up. However, the pages of the Bible began to fly open on their own and turn to different passages. She began to read:

"Death and life are in the power of the tongue: and they that love it shall eat the fruit thereof." - Proverbs 18:21 (KJV)

"As they left Bethany the next day, he was hungry. Off in the distance he saw a fig tree in full leaf. He came up to it expecting to find something for breakfast but found nothing but fig leaves. (It wasn't yet the season for figs.) He addressed the tree: *'No one is going to eat fruit from you again—ever!'*
And his disciples overheard him." -Mark 11:12-14 (MSG)

"In the morning, walking along the road, they saw the fig tree, shriveled to a dry stick. Peter, remembering what had happened the previous day, said to him, <u>'Rabbi, look—the fig tree you cursed is shriveled up!'" -Mark 11:20-21 (MSG)</u>

"God bless America!" I yelled, and everyone looked over at me as though I was crazy. "Death and life," I said. "We can speak about life or death in different situations in our lives. We have nothing to lose but everything to gain."

"Ladies let's hold hands and make a confession that we will take back everything that the enemy stole from us. We will do whatever it takes to break generational curses."

We began to confess prayer bullets from a book called *Prayer Rain*. I obtained it through Boston's Mountain of Fire and Miracles Ministries.

Lord, open doors of opportunity to me through this prayer, in the name of Jesus.

I command all evil unknown forces organized against my life to be scattered, in the name of Jesus.

I paralyze every activity of physical and spiritual parasites and devourers in my life, in the name of Jesus.

Powers denying me my due miracles: receive the stones of fire, in the name of Jesus.

I recover all the ground that I lost to the enemy, in the name of Jesus.

I bind the spirit of depression, frustration, and disillusionment in my life, in the name of Jesus.

Heavenly surgeons, perform the necessary surgical operations in all needed areas of my life, in the name of Jesus.

Lord Jesus, carry out all the repairs that are necessary in my life.

Let all the parasites feeding on any area of my life be roasted, in the name of Jesus.

Fire of God, consume the evil clock of the enemy that is working against my life, in the name of Jesus.

My life is not a fertile ground for any evil to thrive in, in the name of Jesus.

I command that the doors of good things that are closed against me by the enemy be opened, in the name of Jesus.

I reject the spirit of impossibility. I claim opened doors, in the name of Jesus.

I decree restoration sevenfold in weak areas of my life, in the name of Jesus.

I refuse to wage war against myself, unless it is to eradicate seeds of the enemy found within my soul, in the name of Jesus.

Lord, make my case a miracle. Shock my foes, friends, and even myself, in the name of Jesus.

Lord, give me the solution to any problem facing me, in the name of Jesus.

Trees of problems in my life: dry up to the roots, in the name of Jesus.

Walls of physical and spiritual opposition, fall after the order of Jericho, in the name of Jesus.

I possess the power to pursue, overtake and recover my goods from spiritual Egyptians, in the name of Jesus.

Let every spell, jinx, and demonic incantation rendered against me be canceled, in the name of Jesus.

I cancel every effect of any strange help received from Egypt regarding this problem, in the name of Jesus.

Lord, heal all wounds and spiritual bullets sustained from attacks of the enemy, in the name of Jesus.

Let all hidden potentials and gifts that will make me great and those that were stolen from me, be restored twenty-onefold, in the name of Jesus.

I reject the spirit of regret, woes, and disappointment, in the name of Jesus.

Lord, give me power for a new beginning, in the name of Jesus.

Lord, make my life a miracle and be glorified in every area of it, in the name of Jesus.

Lord Jesus, I thank You for answering my prayer.

Then Tracey said, "Guys, if we are going to face Jez, we have to be mentally tough."

Then Fanci added, "Tracey you're right. We need all the help we can get. I think we should plan to fast. We should only allow water since we are out here in this sun, and we need to stay hydrated."

"Well, my sugar drops sometimes, so I'm gonna take some fruit just in case—but only fruit. Yes, that's it. I'll do a fruit fast," Tracey added as she put some bottled water and fresh fruits that she had picked from the garden back into her bag.

"I agree and we could wait to eat 'till sunset. We'll fast during the day until we find Jez. That way we will have all the spiritual ammo we can to take our victory," I said.

"OK guys. We should also pray right now and ask God to give us eyes to see the truth," suggested Tracey, smiling and extending her hands out to me.

Fanci and I looked at each other remembering the violent war I witnessed during the early part of this journey.

"Yes girl," said Fanci, "Tracey you are right again. You can lead the prayer this time."

Tracey reached for the Bible and began to read.

" 'No weapon formed against us shall prosper.' OK, let's close our eyes."

This time Tracey didn't just recite a prayer. This time Tracey prayed, and she started with:

"Our Father, who art in heaven …"

As she finished praying, we all said, "In Jesus' name, Amen."

When we opened our eyes, around us, we were surrounded by bands of angels.

The skies were dark, and there was a violent war going on. Tracey started to shake and said, "Guys, I don't know if I can do this."

"Tracey, yes you can. They have had Doc long enough. You have your angels with you. Put them to work," I said.

With that, I began to speak the words, "I am more than a conqueror," and as the words exited my mouth, I could see the sound begin to take shape into a sword. I grabbed the sword and forged forward.

"You guys, look!" I shouted amongst all the fighting and clashing going on.

"Use your words!" I yelled, and then I saw a demon headed toward me. I swung at it and split it in half.

Though I destroyed it, half my sword was gone. I began to grow in fear, but then I decided to stay in faith. *No matter what, keep going*, I could hear Doc say.

"God has not given us a spirit of fear," I said, and the sound left my mouth and suddenly like a magnet, those words were drawn to my sword. My sword was whole again. I kept pushing, speaking, and praying. As I looked to my left and my right, my friends too were fighting their way down the path. "According to Proverbs 3 v 25, I have no reason to fear sudden disaster or the destruction that comes to the wicked. I can trust the Lord to protect me, and He will not allow me to fall into harm."

There was fire everywhere. Angels and demons were fighting. On the roads beside us, suddenly you could see people being attacked, but because they refused to walk in truth, they couldn't see that they were under attack. Unfortunately, they suffered.

There were demons floating around their heads, grabbing at them, pushing at them and their kids, and some demons were even able to step inside of some people. Their angels just stood there looking at them silently because their assignments did not know how to stand in faith or how to access the strength of their assigned angels.

Then, we saw our very first crosswalk. The street sign read, "Generational Blessing Street."

Generational Blessing Street

"Hey guys, it's working. Keep decreeing. Generational blessings are mine," yelled Fanci as she took the head off a demon. "By the stripes of Jesus, I am healed!" she yelled again.

Then suddenly, a dark mist rose out of her chest, and through tears she kept walking and fighting and staying in faith. "No weapon formed against me shall prosper," I heard her say.

Then I took a hit and fell to the ground. A scary looking figure was sitting on top of me, spitting in my face and saying, "You are nothing. Your mother was nothing. Your sisters are nothing. You are nothing."

Tears began to form in my eyes, and then I yelled, "Ministering angels, come forth now and keep me protected!"

The second my words left my lips, the skies opened, and one hundred more angels began to descend and immediately attack the demon on me. I quickly stood up and continued my fight.

"We are fearfully and wonderfully made. I am the head and not the tail. I am a child of the Most God," I said.

I began to swing my sword with all my might, and I kept moving forward.

"Lord!" I heard Tracey shouting at the top of her lungs.

"Thank you that my family is safe. Thank you that we have more than enough," she said.

Then Fanci stopped and yelled out and said "Guys! Why are we fighting?"

We all stopped and looked at her. Just then a dark figure aggressively headed her way. Tracey released her sword and said, "Get behind me, Satan. In Jesus' name." And with that, the sword began to swing itself back with astonishing power.

We all looked at each other in astonishment, and simultaneously released our own swords and started coming together, walking towards the enemy, and speaking the Word of God. Our swords went ahead of us, doing the fighting for us. All we had to do was stand back and speak forth the Word, and that was the end of it.

Shortly after, all the dark skies cleared up, and the sunshine returned. We decided to sit by a tree to rest and watch the sunset.

"Maybe we could eat some fruit?" Fanci suggested.

"No way. We made a vow, and we haven't even dealt with Jez yet. We gotta be ready," I said. "Well, I hope this fasting thing really works because I'm grateful for this fruit, but I could use some real food right about now," said Tracey.

"It's got to. Listen. Way before I turned to God, I experienced the power it holds. At that time, I was sixteen years old and living with friends. Well, one day one of my friends went to jail. He had come looking for me, but I wasn't home and this was before cell phones. I was worried. A different friend shared with me how her grandmother had taught her how to sacrifice something she enjoyed, to acquire that thing. Like making a trade. Later I would learn this was like a biblical principle called fasting. She instructed me to give up cigarettes for three days and to see what happened. So, I did. Now, I know what one might think: *Cigarettes, really?* But let me tell you that on that third day, my friend in jail had somehow tracked down my phone number and he
did call me from jail. So, I say this, "If it worked then, without me knowing God too well, how much more powerful can this spiritual weapon be now that I do walk with God," I explained.

"Are you kidding?" asked Tracey.

"Not even" I responded and leaned my head back. I began to think about my past. I reflected on how lost and deceived I had been and the unusual ways the enemy had me bound. I also remembered the times God intervened for me and the moments when the chains of lies and deceit had been broken and I was set free. Each step of pursuit after God by way of Jesus

Christ brought on a new level of freedom. The truth was I was created for a purpose and had a destiny preset for me. I was a child of The Most High God. "You are so good God. Thank you, Jesus." I mumbled as I drifted off to sleep, and then dream began:

I was standing up before a surgeon, I had just come out of surgery and I stared at myself. I noticed the surgical errors. Slowly and hesitantly, I spoke up requesting the surgeon fix it, only to be denied. "No, you are OK."

I looked down at it again and a little louder said, "No, I need you to fix it." Again, he denied me.

The more I kindly insisted the more careless his denial became. It was not until my insistence became fused with an angry righteous indignation that I finally got his attention. It was a righteous demand that finally got him to correct the surgical errors.

I slowly opened my eyes, and I stared up at the sky. I would never have thought I would be on this journey. I looked over at Fanci and Tracey as they slept. I turned over face flat on the ground. Giving God thanks, asking Him to protect us and guide our path. I had no idea how we were gonna find Jez, but we had to get Doc back and take her out.

As I became quiet and tried to listen. I began to think about the dream. God had used this dream to show me that I had to demand what I wanted in life with the authority of Jesus Christ. I had to learn how to exercise my authority when the physical rights I was blessed with, under my spiritual covenant with Jesus, were being violated. I began to grow angry and sat up.

We would find Doc. We would complete our journey. Righteous indignation began to grow within me. "Guys get up. Let's go! We're gonna get our friend back!"

Righteous indignation is a kind of holy anger that stems from a perception of a wrong being done or an injustice. It is knowing who we are in Christ and fiercely coming up against anything that threatens our rights or our blessings. When I envision this term, I see cops busting into a house and taking my family without any Miranda rights or explanation and not telling me where they are being taken. I would be fighting with every bit of life I had. This is how we are to take a stance when the enemy comes for what is ours by right of Christ. No, we don't fight against people. We take the injustice and enter into the courts of heaven and there we lay our case down at The Throne. But if we don't enter the courts of heaven, how can we expect to seek His Hand in the matters of our life? He died to give us an abundant life, spilling over. Not just OK. Not just money. Not just health. Not just love. Every area. His desire and His Will for us is to have an abundant and prosperous life in all areas.

3 John 1v2:

Beloved, I wish above all things that thou mayest prosper and be in health, even as thy soul prosperity. John 10v10:

The thief cometh not, but for to steal, and to kill, and to destroy; I am come that they might have life, and that they might have it more abundantly.

Psalm 100V4

Enter into his gates with thanksgiving; And into his courts with praise.

Isaiah 43V26

Review the past for me, let us argue the matter together, state the case for your innocence

As everyone gathered their bags, we began to lean in on the power of our words to inspire us and begin the spiritual assault against our enemies.

'I am an overcomer. I am the head and not the tail. I am courageous. I am strong. I am loved. I will win. The fight is rigged.'

Soon we were on our way again—and as we continued, we realized the street names had changed some.

"Ladies, look," I said as I pointed to a sign that read 'Expiration Date,' the wording began to change to 'Expected Desire.'

"Yes," said Fanci, "it's working."

We all began to run in excitement.

As we continued on our path, it suddenly began to grow dark again, but we were nowhere near sunset.

"Guys, I think we are getting closer," Tracey said.

Ahead behind a huge bush of thistles, we could see an abandoned warehouse. I had the most horrible feeling.

"What is going on here?" I asked. I immediately started to pray in tongues. I didn't understand, and I needed the Holy Ghost to intervene.

We prayed as we continued to walk up to the front of the warehouse. There stood a big black door, and the windows were covered with black tint.

"Do we knock or just bust in the door?" said Fanci.

I touched the knob to turn it, and it was unlocked. I pulled back my hand.

"What happened?" asked Fanci.

"It's not even locked, Fanci. What if this is a trap?" I asked.

"We have come all of this way, and we are not turning back now," said Fanci as she stepped forward and turned the doorknob herself.

"Yeah, yeah." I said as I followed her in.

There comes a time in your life when you become tired of living in defeat and fear. As we headed down the hallway, feeling our way through by gripping and feeling the sides of the wall we reached another door and as I turned the knob, witnessed the most unforeseen image. Our mouths dropped as we saw Jez and all her minions lying flat-faced on the ground. No movement. No life.

I was in awe at what I had seen. It reminded me of when Jehoshaphat and his men found their enemies dead upon arrival.

2 Chronicles 20:15-30 ERV

Jahaziel said, "Listen to me King Jehoshaphat and everyone living in Judah and Jerusalem! The LORD says this to you: 'Don't be afraid or worry about this large army, because the battle is not your battle. It is God's battle! Tomorrow, they will come up through the Ziz Pass. You must go down to them. You will find them at the end of the valley on the other side of the desert of Jeruel. You will not have to fight this battle. Just stand there and watch the LORD save you. Judah and Jerusalem, don't be afraid. Don't worry because the LORD is with you. So go out to stand against those people tomorrow.'" Jehoshaphat bowed with his face to the ground. And all the people of Judah and Jerusalem bowed down before the LORD and worshiped him. The Levites from the Kohath family groups, and the Korah family stood up to praise the LORD, the God of Israel. They sang very loudly. Early the next morning, Jehoshaphat's army went out into the desert of Tekoa. As they marched out, Jehoshaphat stood there saying, "Listen to me, men of Judah and Jerusalem. Have faith in the LORD your God, and you will stand strong! Have faith in his prophets, and you will succeed!" Jehoshaphat encouraged the men and gave them instructions. Then he had the Temple singers stand up in their special clothes to praise the LORD. They marched in front of the army and sang, "Give thanks to the LORD! His faithful love will last forever."

As they began to sing and to praise God, the LORD set an ambush for the army from Ammon, Moab, and Mount Seir who had come to attack Judah. The enemy was defeated! The Ammonites and the Moabites started to fight the men from Mount Seir. After they killed them, the Ammonites and Moabites turned on themselves and killed each other. The men from Judah arrived at the lookout point in the desert. They looked for the enemy's large army, but all they saw were dead bodies lying on the ground. There were no survivors. Jehoshaphat and his army came to take things from the bodies. They found many animals, riches, clothes, and other valuable things. It was more than Jehoshaphat and his men could carry away. There was so much that they spent three days taking everything from the dead bodies. On the fourth day Jehoshaphat and his army met in the Valley of Beracah. They praised the LORD. That is why people still call that place, "The Valley of Beracah." All the men from Judah and Jerusalem were very happy as they marched back to Jerusalem with Jehoshaphat in the front. The LORD made them very happy when he defeated their enemy. They entered Jerusalem with lyres, harps, and trumpets and went to the Temple of the LORD. People in all the surrounding kingdoms became afraid of God when they heard that the LORD fought against the enemies of Israel. That is why there was peace for

Jehoshaphat's kingdom—his God brought him rest from the enemies that were all around him.

We stood and looked at the bodies for a couple of minutes, holding our noses. We began to open all the windows to allow in the cool breeze and light to enter in, then we began thoroughly searching for Doc. It was a fruitless search. We decided to head back out and regroup. It was a bittersweet feeling. On one hand we were excited about Jez's defeat. On the other, there were no signs of Doc. As we sat down discouraged, we began to hear a soft melody. "He will make a way, You always make a way." It was a song by Elevation, Make A Way. "We need help guys," said Tracey, "I did hear once that when the praises go up the blessings come down."

We began to sing along with the melody. Sweetly our praises rose, and our focus became Jesus. I closed my eyes and just began to give Him thanks and then suddenly I looked over to my right and I saw a black robe sticking out from underneath the bushes. I placed my finger over my lips, as I nudged the girls and pointed over to the bushes. They continued singing as I got up and walked over.

    I jumped behind the bush and the robed old man was so startled he threw my tote up in the air. He held his hands up in the air and began to cry out loud and apologize. Fanci and Tracey ran over to us.

"I am so sorry." Jez made me do it. He sat down, buried his face in his hands and continued to cry.

"Ahem, ladies. Hello?" we heard Doc saying from my bag.

"Doc!" The three of us said simultaneously.

"Well, it's about time ladies. Now let me explain, I wasn't ever worried. These guys were the ones who had something to be worried about," he said looking over towards the factory. "You see Ladies, I have an anointing on my life that makes me a threat to their kingdom and can't nobody just "handle" me without severe consequences sanctioned by Mr. El, Himself. The minute anybody not of God touches me they are stricken with a curse and some even death. Actually, ladies, Jez and her minions have been dead for quite some time. That is why the stench is so odiferous. The minute they tried to handle me they were all smote by the Power of the Holy Spirit Himself. This guy here was the only one shown mercy because he was willing to help me look for you three. When we heard you singing we headed back, but when he saw you, he got scared and decided to hide." Doc began to shake his head.

"Well Doc, he tried to bully us and almost put us on the wrong path," I said as I kicked his foot.

"G,G., apologize, more importantly forgive." Doc said.

"You have to believe that in this journey we are on, everyone is doing the best they know how. He only knew Jez and that's what he learned to do. Then learned a way, and now he will meet Mr. El. When you know better you do better. That is what this journey is about. Forgive, G.G.

I looked over at Fanci and Tracey. Fanci shrugged and Tracey smiled. "Fine Doc, but if he tries anything else." I threatened.

"He won't," Doc said, and the robed man chimed in "I won't"

The robed man slowly rose and began to dust himself off. "Now I can get rid of this ugly back robe" He said and yanked off the black robe.
Underneath he revealed a pristine baby blue suit. "My name is Derek," he said as he used one hand to adjust his hair and the other he held out to shake my hand.

The three of us looked at each other and then at his hand. Astonished at his transformation we each took turns shaking his hand. "I know. It's a long story. Have you ever heard of the saying 'if you can't beat them, join them?' Well, that is what happened to me. We can talk about it on the way but thank you so much for sticking to your journey because now you have helped me complete mine, which was to get to Mr. El."

After a few more words, we began to sing and praise as we began on our journey again. We couldn't wait to get back to Mr. El. We had Doc back, and soon we would be reunited with Grover. Then we would be going home. My heart was overflowing with joy. As we walked, birds started flying by and dropping off drinks and food that we accepted graciously. We walked for a long while, talking and sharing different moments of our lives back home. That night as we huddled near each other , we slept peacefully under the tree with the smell of Wild Jasmine surrounding us once again. "God I trust you," I whispered and closed my eyes for the night.

In the morning, we awoke, and we were surrounded by fresh fruit and bread. After praying and reading some scripture, we ate some breakfast and we continued our journey.

Chapter 12

Homecoming

Time went by quickly. When we arrived, we saw Gabriel smiling, standing there as if he had been waiting. He opened the door for us, and he let us into the lovely, bright, and incredible castle. We returned to Mr. El's room.

Carefully placing our goggles on we excitedly waited for Mr. El. As we heard the door open my heart began to beat faster. He walked toward us smiling. "Doc my old friend, it is so good to see you again."

Doc smiled big "It is always a pleasure Mr. El. No one else I would rather be in service in,"

"I'm glad to hear you say that because I am sending you out on another mission this very night," said Mr. El.

"As for the rest of you, Great accomplishment! Now go in peace," He said and started walking away with a smile. We all looked at each other.

"Mr. El.one moment, please. You said that if we went back and took Jez head on, we would get everything that was taken," I said.

"Tell me again what it is that you were looking for?" He asked, almost smiling.

"Well, I was in search of my identity," I said.

"And you mean to tell me that after all this, you still don't know who you are?" Mr. El inquired.

I couldn't reply because He was right. It was clearer than it had ever been in my life.

"You wouldn't have been able to stand up to Jez and break generational curses if you weren't sure of your identity. Fasting, prayers and confessions are connected to your identity. Each one of your problems was connected to your identity.

"Fanci, as a child of God, you have every right to be healed. Since you know who you are now and your identity has been revealed, you will walk in wholeness. You have learned the true meaning of righteous indignation. You are cancer-free.

Tracey, because you know your identity now, you know that you are valuable, and you don't deserve the abuse you have been taking for the past years. You don't have to fear anymore. You can let that go and since you have discovered the Ultimate True Love you can start to expect real love again. Nothing will be too hard for you. No matter how dark a season is, you will be a lighthouse to those who are lost.

G.G., you have been through a lot, but now you know that your identity is not simply connected to your natural family, but it is ultimately connected to Christ. You are a daughter of God, and you are truly blessed and highly favored. Everything your heart, hand, or foot touch will prosper, and your story will bring many to The Throne.

Now it is time for all of you to live out your lives by walking in your true identities," said Mr. El.

Then Gabriel drew near to me and handed me a sword. It was gold and sparkly.

"Now the journey continues, and it is time for you to fight. You're fighting not just for yourselves but for others as well. You will fight for the weak, the poor, the broken-hearted and so many more. You are now soldiers in my army. You fight for The Lord of Hosts," Mr. El said firmly.

My eyes began to water again because I knew exactly what He meant, but this time I wasn't afraid. I knew that I had the best army on the planet backing me, and the best leader who had my best interest at heart; one that I could call Father.

Then Grover walked in the room. I couldn't describe the expression on his face. Peace? Sadness? Joy? I couldn't discern it.

"Mr. El has requested I stay on...here, just a little bit longer."

Our mouths dropped.

"I'll be able to do so much more from here," he said as he stared at all three of us, "Mr. El has shown me so much here. I can't even begin to explain how it is here," he said with a little more excitement.

"Grover..." I began to question but then he spoke up.

"Guys, I am miraculously healed, here. I need more time. I did a trial run out there, and I'm not ready. I was still struggling, even to walk. The air is so easy here. I can breathe. I'm running. I am grateful for you, but I'm staying, just a little bit longer" he said and hugged each of us again.

Then Derek raised his manicured hand, "Mr. El, could I stay on a little longer too?" Mr. El nodded and smiled.

"Well, Mr. El, how do we get back home?" I asked.

"You have to go back the way you came from once again, but this time in the fullness of who you are," said Mr. El.

That night, we prayed with Doc as he left for his next mission, and we laughed and feasted. We enjoyed having Grover in our midst, even if just for those moments. I knew it was for the better, but that fact wasn't making it easier.

Later as I laid my head on the pillow, I prayed again and gave God my concern about leaving our friend behind, and in the morning, my spirit had lifted. I had appreciated the time we had with Grover, but I was also excited about getting back home. As we walked out the front door, we waved our goodbyes to everyone.

Grover said, "It's not goodbye. It's see you later," as he closed the door behind him.

This time we were ready and so we continued our journey.

Happily Ever After

We all continued to talk about what we were going to do differently once we got home.

Soon we came up to our first cross street. It was called "Happily Ever After," and Tracey grew excited. As we looked over at Tracey, we could see her bruises visibly begin to heal. She looked down at her arms and moved them—palms up, palms down—and smiled as she too noticed her bruises fading. Tracey looked down the street and could see herself sitting on the front porch of a very large house. She was staring out into the road, daydreaming, and partially watching her children play safely in the leaves she had just raked into a pile. A handsome dark-haired man came through the front door and wrapped his arms around her.

"Hey honey, I love you," he said. Tracey warmly smiled.

She looked back at us. "You guys, thank you!" Then she waved as she ran down the street toward her destiny.

"Let's go, girl. I am ready." Fanci said.

"Yeah, and I'd like us to hurry up before night falls upon us," I added.

"Good point. Let's hurry," I said.

We both began to walk briskly. Although it had only been a day, I felt more spiritually prepared. I was noticing certain things, and more signs were changing. Street names appeared such as "No More Cards," "Abuse No More," "Loving
Parents," and "Broken Curses."

Suddenly, we saw a woman sitting on the side of the road with spirits surrounding her, whispering into her ears. She remained balled up with her face tucked into her jacket. Fanci and I stared at each other and quickly ran up to her. "I rebuke you in the name of Jesus Christ. Get outta here!" Fanci and I yelled.

The gaseous figures looked up and screeched, but quickly dissipated.

"Hey, are you OK?" Fanci asked.

The woman looked up at us with big, beautiful brown eyes and said, "Yeah, I think so. But I really just want to be left alone."

She covered her face again. "Hi, my name is G.G. What's your name?" I asked.

She looked up again and said, "Marci. My name is Marci."

"Well, you don't have to be afraid, Marci. We aren't going to hurt you," I said.

"I'm not afraid," she said, sitting up. "I just don't like people. I've learned you can't trust them."

I looked at her and said, "Not everyone is like that, Marci."

Then Fanci and I looked at each other and laughed out loud. "Actually ... OK, a lot of people are like that—but not everyone. What are you doing here?" I asked.

She said, "I was on a flight back home from Germany, when my husband called to tell me he was divorcing me. Honestly, my whole life I've tried to do the right thing. I've always been honest. I've always tried to treat people well despite being mistreated. But the only thing I've ever wanted was a family—my family—and to be loved." She started crying, and I hugged her.

She continued, "I remember going to sleep and when I woke up, I was the only one on my plane. When I got off, I ended up here. I met this woman named Stacia, and she told me to find Mr. El and to stay on this particular path. But really, it's too hard and too confusing, and I just want to be left alone. It's easier to just stay here and stay to myself, in my own world." She pulled herself away and hid her face again.

"Marci, I can tell by looking in your eyes that you are a good person and have a good heart, and these things you want ... you can have them. But you have to get back up and continue your journey. If you don't, you are just going to stay stuck here. I will walk with you, but you have to get up."

"No, I'm fine here. There's no point. Please leave me alone. I don't care anymore," she replied.

"Marci, I can really help. We can do this together. You don't have to stay here. Please join us," I pleaded. But Marci would not move.

I tried for a few more minutes. Then Fanci said, "Uhhh, G.G. look over at that street sign." I looked over to the right and could see a street sign named, "The Last Tear," but the street and the signs looked as if they were disappearing.

Fanci took a deep breath and said, "That's me. I have to go." She yanked off her pink handkerchief, and we could see her hair visibly growing back before our eyes.

"Thank you, Mr. El. THANK YOU JESUS!" she whispered as she looked up at the sky.

We both looked to the right onto the street and saw Fanci coloring a mannequin's head of hair in a classroom setting.

"I guess it's beauty school for me," said Fanci with a huge smile on her face because she had a vision of what was to come.

She hugged me as she wiped a solid tear from her face and then looked at Marci. "Marci, you've got to want the change, to receive the change."

She turned to me. "You got this, G.G. Be strong!" she said as she threw up deuces and ran off to her destiny. "My friend, I love you. Thank you."

And there I stood, alone with Marci. "Marci, come with me. Let's do this together."

Initially, Marci continued to decline but I was persistent. As the light began to slip away, I looked around the area and began to hear noises in the trees beginning to draw closer and continued to encourage her.

"Marci, we have to leave soon."

Then suddenly, she looked up and agreed to join me.

As we walked, I reflected on this entire journey. Though I didn't know what was to come, I knew that I was ready. I held onto my sword, knowing I was ready to fight for my predestined life and for that of my family.

Self-Acceptance

Shortly after, we came across a street called "Self-Acceptance." On this street, I saw myself sitting at a table autographing books. I shared stories of struggle and overcoming. It was no longer about caring what others thought; it was about me accepting myself, doing better and becoming who God had ultimately created me to be. I looked over at Marci and we locked elbows.

"You ready?" I asked Marci and she nodded yes. "Doc, are you ready?"

"I am always prepared young lady," replied Doc.

Just before I stepped onto the road, I turned around and looked all around me at the beauty and splendor. As we took our first step, I stopped for a moment. "Thank you God. Thank you Jesus. Thank you Holy Spirit."

I knew that this was only the beginning of my journey to a brighter future, and then...our journey continued.

Acknowledgements

I would like to thank God, Jesus, and The Holy Spirit for all the divine assistance, intervention and guidance my entire life. I love you.

I thank my mother, Teresa deJesus Gonzalez, for her love, for teaching me the importance of kindness, and showing me the importance of always finding a way to laugh.

I would like to thank my father, Napoleon Gonzalez, for the gift of intelligence.

I thank every single Teacher, Pastor, Evangelist, Prophet and Apostle who has ever poured into my life or come to support me in my time of need.

I thank every single teacher, principal and professor who taught and helped to guide my mind.

I thank David and Daisy Hernandez for always believing in me and fighting for all of us, but especially me.

I thank the Arias family for ushering me into The Kingdom and for all of your love and support.

I thank Eugene and Cheryl Basey for their support and love in my vulnerable years.

I thank Gloria Hall for your love, Grace, and support during my vulnerable years.

Special thanks to every single one of my friends who stood by me no matter what.

Special thanks to my greatly talented niece. Evangenlina Salazar for the illustration the rose.

You are all appreciated.

About The Author

Guadalupe Gonzalez was partially raised in a small city, near the southmost part of Texas, named Harlingen. There she began her beginnings in the Lemoyne Gardens Housing Community but soon was transplanted to Lansing, Michigan, where she would finish her childhood and go on to achieve her degree in nursing. Also, in this season she began a very intimate walk with Jesus Christ, it was then she learned how to apply The Word of God to overcome in life. Her desire is to revive hope and help others realign themselves with Gods plan for their life by applying The Living Word and standing on His Promises. Guadalupe's message is that we are all destined to win, according to Romans 8v28.

She currently resides in Houston, Texas and works as an emergency room nurse. She enjoys spreading Gods love and the knowledge of Jesus Christ to everyone she encounters.

Made in the USA
Columbia, SC
26 March 2024